THE COMPLETE BOOK
of
HANUKKAH

THE COMPLETE BOOK

of

HANUKKAH

by **KINNERET CHIEL**

illustrated by **ARNOLD LOBEL**

KTAV PUBLISHING HOUSE, INC.

Library of Congress Cataloging in Publication Data

Chiel, Kinneret, ed.
  The complete book of Hanukkah.

  Reprint of the 1959 ed. published by Friendly House
Publishers, New York.
  Bibliography: p.
  1. Hanukkah (Feast of Lights)—Juvenile literature.
I. Title.
BM695.H3C5 1976   296.4'35   75-40464
ISBN 0-87068-367-5

PREFACE

In recent years Hanukkah has become a major festival for Jews in the Western world. One of the reasons for this development was discussed with great understanding almost half a century ago by Justice Louis D. Brandeis of the Supreme Court of the United States.

Justice Brandeis in an address delivered in Boston in 1912, characterized Hanukkah as "a victory of democracy over aristocracy, . . . a struggle in which all Americans, non-Jews as well as Jews, should be vitally interested because they are vitally affected."

"Courage, hope, enthusiasm, devotion and self-sacrifice of the plain people"—these, Justice Brandeis believed, were the qualities of the Jews who resisted the Syrian tyranny and made possible the Maccabean victory, and these were the secret of their eternal youth.

If these are the ingredients for a nation which is eternally youthful they are also the very ones which shaped our own young America. They are in fact the qualities of youth everywhere—heroic, truthful and strong!

It is perhaps for this reason that Hanukkah has become a favorite festival of American Jewish youth, a time for gaiety and grateful celebration. We, the editor and publishers believe that a holiday so important to youth deserves special treatment in a book particularly designed for young people.

And so offered here side by side within the covers of one book are history, poetry, legend, story and song—all about Hanukkah. It is our hope that young people who come to look will stay to browse and read, and will finally find within these covers a complete picture of the Feast of Lights, of Hanukkah.

I should like to express my gratitude to those who in one way or another helped this book on its way; to the publishers, Bernard and Sol Scharfstein for their friendship and for their encouragement; to Rabbi I. Edward Kiev, Librarian, Jewish Institute of Religion— Hebrew Union College, who kindly provided me with necessary source material; to the Israeli Consulate, the Zionist Archives and the library of the Jewish Education Committee for making their library facilities available to me; to Mr. Harry Coopersmith, of The Jewish Education Committee, Cantor Moshe Nathanson, Mr. Benjamin Stambler and Mr. Oscar Tarcov, who were good enough to answer my questions and offered helpful advice; to Miss Ilana Grynbaum who gave me information about Hanukkah in Israel; to Mr. David Goldberg of the Theodor Herzl Institute who was kind enough to direct my steps to an excellent source for materials; to Mrs. Hetty Applebaum, a most gracious lady, who generously and cheerfully typed the manuscript. Finally I should like to thank my husband Rabbi Arthur Chiel for his constant assistance and encouragement. During the months which it took to compile this book his patience was unlimited and his enthusiasm often exceeded my own.

KINNERET CHIEL
Tuckahoe, N. Y.
November, 1959

To my children,

Deborah
Danny
Naomi
and
David

CONTENTS

Acknowledgements

The editor and publisher gratefully acknowledge their debt to a number of individuals and organizations who graciously granted permission to reprint material from other publications. Sincere thanks are extended to:

Acum Ltd., of Tel Aviv, Israel for permission to use the Hebrew texts by L. Kipnis for the songs, "S'vivon," "Hanukkah, Chag Yafeh Kol Kach"

American Judaism, official publication of The Union of American Hebrew Congregations, for permission to reprint Budd Schulberg's "Reflections on Hanukkah and the American Struggle for Independence."

Budd Schulberg—for permission to use his "Reflections on Hanukkah and the American Struggle for Independence."

Crown Publishers, for permission to reprint the translation by Frances and Julius Butwin of "Chanukah Money" by Sholem Aleichem, from the book, "The Old Country."

David Einhorn for permission to reprint his story "Reb Yudel's Hanukkah" which appeared in World Over, issue of November 28, 1947.

Jewish Publication Society of America for permission to reprint the poems, "Blessings for Hanukkah" by Jessie E. Sampter, "My Hanukkah Candles" by Philip M. Raskin and "Hasmonean Lights" by J. Fichman, which appeared in the book "Hanukkah" by Emily Solis-Cohen.

Sol Klein for permission to reprint the story "Reuben Lights a Torah" which appeared in World Over, issue of December 13, 1946.

Rufus Learsi for permission to reprint his poem "Hail the Maccabees."

Dr. Lee J. Levinger for permission to reprint two poems by Elma Ehrlich Levinger. These are "Mattathias" and "Before the Menorah."

The Nahum Nardi Music Foundation for permission to reprint Mr. Nardi's song "Kemah Kemah."

Rabbi Leon Spitz for permission to reprint his story "A Hanukkah Night in Old Philadelphia."

The Union of American Hebrew Congregations for permission to reprint Elma Ehrlich Levinger's poem "Judas Maccabeus to His Soldiers" which appeared in Mrs. Levinger's book "Chanukah Entertainments."

Reflections on Hanukkah and the American Struggle for Independence

Every time we observe Hanukkah we experience a new birth of freedom. As a Jew, as an American and as a writer, I have three good reasons for knowing just how precious that freedom is.

*   *   *   *   *   *

Hanukkah reminds us that Jews came here as "ready-made citizens," in the sense that our history was preparing us for the free atmosphere of American life for thousands of years. Indeed, Judaism helped to create America. It was one of the great tributaries flowing into the broad river of this nation's idealism. Without Judaism and its emphasis on reverence for the individual, there could have been no Jefferson, no Declaration of Independence, no Constitution.

*   *   *   *   *

When I think of the Maccabean struggle, I think of the way it was paralleled by our own American revolution.

Mattathias was Tom Paine, Ben Franklin and Sam Adams gathered into one towering figure.

There were many "Boston Massacres," as the Judeans resisted the Syrian demands that idolatry reign supreme.

The small band of Maccabeans courageously defied the agents of foreign rule. They staged many a Boston Tea Party.

*   *   *   *   *   *

At West Point there is a bas-relief of Judah Maccabee in a panel of great warriors. His picture belongs there. He was the Washington of the Maccabean saga. His men were as ragged as the miserable company at Valley Forge. Like Washington, Judah saw many of them desert and he sustained the morale of the others with his courage. Said Judah to his followers: "They come against us in much pride and iniquity . . . We fight for our lives and our precepts. . ."

*   *   *   *   *   *

The forces under Judah outmaneuvered the invader. Thousands of Syrian footmen, we read in the Books of the Maccabees, crept up on Judah's camp at night, but Judah had already moved his men into the mountains. Then suddenly he appeared in force on the plains and won a great battle. It was their Saratoga.

*   *   *   *   *   *

Against the Syrian general, Seron, Judah launched a surprise attack. It was not unlike the famous crossing of the Delaware which enabled Washington to catch the German mercenaries off guard at Trenton.

When Antiochus sent fresh troops against Judah, his men desperately called upon God: "How shall we be able to stand together except Thou be our help?" Compare this to Jefferson's cry, "We devoutly implore the assistance of Almighty God to deliver us from the evils of civil war."

Judah declared: "It is better for us to die in battle than to behold the calamities of our people and our sanctuary." Doesn't Patrick Henry's famous, "Give me liberty or give me death!" sound like an echo of Judah's utterance?

*   *   *   *   *   *

The Judeans found some compensation for the black horror of war in the feeling that they had protected something precious for future generations. The legend of the light that endured I take as a poetic symbol of freedom's power of survival if it is energetically protected.

When we celebrate Hanukkah, we honor both the traditions of Judaism and reinvigorate the principles of Americanism.

BUDD SCHULBERG

Hanukkah in History

The Festival of Hanukkah tells a story of unbelievable courage and faith. It shows how a passion for religious liberty enabled a small people to fight against tremendous odds, and to wrest its freedom from a mighty empire. It is an exciting and inspiring story.

This is how it happened.

In 336 B.C.E., a hundred and fifty years before the Hanukkah story really began, Alexander the Great became King of Macedonia and Greece. Although he was then only twenty years old the young king was already a brilliant general and before long he had conquered some of the oldest civilizations of the ancient world. The Greeks soon ruled the near east, western Asia and northern Africa — in short much of the then known world.

One of the smallest and least significant states of the Grecian world empire was the tiny kingdom of Judea. It lay between two giant powers, Egypt to the south and Syria to the north, and was surrounded on all sides by countries who had succumbed to Greek culture. This culture came to be known as *Hellenism*. Everywhere in the towns of Western Asia people began to speak Greek and to take on the outward appearance of Greeks. Only in Judea did the people continue to live a separate and distinctive way of life.

Upon Alexander's death in 323 B.C.E., his empire was divided among his generals. Syria, Judea's northern neighbor, fell to Seleucus who established the Seleucid dynasty. Egypt, Judea's southern neighbor fell under the control of Ptolemy. Judea, though small and poor, was the corridor which linked Asia and Africa. Through it troops could be moved from one continent to another. The trade routes of commerce and caravans cut across it from east to west and from north to south. So it was a highly prized territory and was buffeted back and forth between its greedy neighbors for generations. Finally in 198 B.C.E. Judea was conquered by the Syrian monarch, Antiochus the Great.

For a time Judea was permitted to live in peace. In hundreds of villages the people tilled the soil, tended their vineyards and took their sheep to graze in the hills. Like their fathers before them they studied the Law, the Torah, and tried to live a good and just life.

This was not a large country nor was it rich. There were no great fertile plains to farm; rough hills and narrow valleys broke up the land in all directions. Jerusalem, its chief city, was the holy city. It too did not support a life of ease and luxury.

But the people of Judea loved their land for its wild uneven beauty and for the good and simple life it gave them. And they were content.

Then in 175 B.C.E. Antiochus Epiphanes ascended the throne of Syria. He was an ambitious, restless man who dreamed of building a great empire just as Alexander the Great had done a hundred and fifty years before. So hungry was he for power and fame that he declared himself the living incarnation of the Greek god Zeus. He demanded that his subjects everywhere prove their loyalty to him by worshipping Zeus. To dramatize this mad idea he stamped coins on which his own portrait represented Zeus.

Pursuing his dream of one great empire, Antiochus demanded that the peoples under his rule abandon their own customs and ideas and accept Greek culture and practices. In Judea his first move was to depose Onias, the High Priest, a loyal Jew, and to install in his place his brother Joshua who sympathized with the Greeks. Joshua changed his name to Jason and proceeded to open Jerusalem to the influence of Hellenism.

Under his direction, a Greek style gymnasium was constructed in the Holy City. Young priests were urged to forget their duties in the Temple and to engage in Greek sports. A small group of Jews from the wealthy upper class was dazzled by Hellenism and especially by its outward trappings. Following Jason's example they assumed Greek names and adopted Greek dress and Greek ways. Some of them even suggested that the God of Israel and Zeus might be worshipped side by side. For this had long since become the practice of the heathen peoples of Antiochus' domains.

But most Jews would not exchange their belief in one God and in the traditions of their fathers for a foreign culture and a heathen god. Infuriated that this small stubborn people should stand in his way, Antiochus became obsessed with the idea of converting the population of Judea into Zeus-worshipping Greeks. He marched into Jerusalem, defiled the Temple and slaughtered hundreds of faithful Jews. Then he issued a decree that the Temple be turned into a shrine of Zeus, and that sacrifices of forbidden animals be brought on the

3

altar to the Greek god. From that time forward, he decreed, any Jew found observing the Jewish Law in any form or manner should be put to death.

Jews were forbidden to observe the Sabbath, to circumcise their sons, to study the Law. They were ordered to eat foods forbidden them by Jewish law and to sacrifice upon heathen altars which sprang up in every village and town in Judea. The officers of Antiochus and his mercenaries appeared throughout the land to enforce the king's decrees. Instead of Greek culture they brought bloodshed and death. It was a tragic hopeless time for this small and weak people.

But suddenly the people arose!

It began in the village of Modin, where Mattathias the Hasmonean lived with his five stalwart sons, John, Simon, Judah, Eleazar and Jonathan. When the King's officers came to Modin they summoned Mattathias, for he was a prominent citizen in the village. With honeyed words of flattery and promises of honor and wealth, they asked Mattathias to be the first to sacrifice to Zeus, so that others might follow his example. His answer was:

"God forbid that we should forsake the law and ordinances. We will not hearken to the King's words to go from our religion either on the right hand or the left."

Immediately after this daring declaration another Jew approached the altar to do the King's command. Mattathias, his zeal aroused, slew him at the altar. Then he and his sons fled to the hills.

There among the caves and rocks of the Judean wilderness they were joined by more and more brave men, determined to resist the Syrian tyrant. They formed a small army under the leadership of Mattathias, by now an old man. Not long afterward, Mattathias died and his third son, Judah Maccabee, became the new leader of the revolt.

The men under Judah's command were not trained for war. They were farmers, craftsmen, teachers, simple men of peace. Certainly they were no match for the well trained mercenaries of the Syrians. But they had courage and strong convictions. While the hired soldiers of the Syrians fought for money, the Jews fought for their liberty. Their love of liberty was their most powerful weapon!

Armed with this weapon and with a detailed knowledge of the country, Judah led his men in a series of brilliant guerrilla raids. He attacked from the hills under cover of night. He used his knowledge of the terrain to trap the Syrian soldiers in swamps and valleys. He moved swiftly and boldly against the enemy. So great a threat did he and his guerrilla band become that Antiochus sent out a regular army against him under the general, Appolonius. Judah killed Appolonius, defeated his army and thereafter used his captured sword in battle. In the same year he defeated a second army under the command of Seron.

By now the Syrian authorities realized that here was a force to be reckoned with seriously. Determined to crush the Jews for all time, they sent still another army, large and well equipped and led by two famous Syrian generals, Gorgias and Nicanor. The Syrians were so certain of victory that they even permitted slave dealers to join their marching armies. These came with chains and coffers of gold, ready to buy slaves from among the thousands of Jews who, they believed, would be captured on the battlefield.

Judah met the splendid armies of Gorgias and Nicanor on the Judean plain near the town of Emmaus and defeated them soundly. From the booty his army, by now 10,000 strong, provided itself with ample supplies and proper equipment. When in the following year Antiochus sent still a fourth army against him, Judah was ready. Again he scored a brilliant victory, this time near Bethsura in the south. The Syrian troops were shredded to bits and fled to Antioch, the Syrian capital, to lick their wounds.

After three years of fighting and four decisive victories Judah and his army were able to clear Judea of the Syrians. They then took possession of Jerusalem, cleansed the Temple of all the Syrian abominations, and rededicated it to the worship of the Lord God of Israel. The Feast of Rededication was held on the 25th day of Kislev, three years after the Syrians had defiled it, probably in 165 B.C.E. (Historians cannot say with accuracy which is the exact year of the first *Hanukkah*. Most agree that is was 165 B.C.E. or 164 B.C.E.).

However, this important victory did not mark the end of the wars for the Jews. For several years they continued to fight for their freedom and for their very lives. Then Antiochus died and there was a scramble for the Syrian throne among several powerful generals. One of them, Lysias, was fighting in Judea at the time. To strengthen his claim it was necessary for him to return to Syria as quickly as possible. He therefore concluded a peace treaty with Judah in the name of the Syrian government and he restored religious freedom to the Jews. With this act the original aim of the Maccabean uprising was finally achieved.

But the Maccabees were not entirely satisfied. They now desired complete political independence. They fought to free their country of Syrian domination and they were victorious. But in the struggles which followed Judah, and later Jonathan, lost their lives. It remained for Simon, the last of the sons of Mattathias to usher in a new era for Judea.

In 142 B.C.E. when Simon succeeded his brother Jonathan as commander-in-chief of the army, he was appointed High Priest and head of the community. He did in fact become the ruler of the country and established the Hasmonean dynasty of the newly independent kingdom.

For the first time in more than four hundred years since Nebuchadnezzar had exiled Zechariah, the last Judean king, to Babylonia, a Jewish ruler reigned over a free and sovereign kingdom in Judea. The Maccabean uprising had gained a double victory. Political freedom had now been added to religious freedom for the Jews.

Since the time of the Maccabees the battle for religious freedom has been fought over and over again throughout the world. After each victory grateful men and women have dedicated themselves and their traditions to remember the miracle of freedom. Jews remember by observing the Festival of Hanukkah each year anew. Wherever they may be they light candles and retell the story of Judah Maccabee and the glorious miracles of Hanukkah.

Hanukkah Today

Hanukkah in our time is one of the happiest festivals on the Jewish calendar. It comes in the middle of the winter, during the month of December, when the days are cold and harsh. Into this bleak month Hanukkah brings warmth and light and happiness. Homes are filled with a bright holiday spirit; special songs are sung; particular foods are eaten; and candlelight glows in every home.

For Hanukkah like many other Jewish holidays, is a family festival and is celebrated with great gaiety in the home! Often the children decorate the house for Hanukkah. They paste gay paper menorahs on doors and windows; they hang dreydels from the ceiling; and everywhere a menorah and a box of colored candles stand ready for the first night of Hanukkah.

On that night the family gathers round the menorah to participate in the candle-lighting ceremony. The father lights the first candle of the festival week with the *shamash*, the helping candle, and he recites the blessings. If he is in good voice he may sing them for there is a beautiful melody which is traditional for the Hanukkah blessings.

Here are the blessings for the Hanukkah candle-lighting ceremony.

"Blessed art Thou, O Lord, our God, Ruler of the universe, Who has sanctified us by Thy commandments and commanded us to kindle the light of Hanukkah.

"Blessed art Thou, O Lord, our God, Ruler of the universe, who performed miracles for our forefathers, in those days, at this season."

These are followed by well loved hymns, such as *Haneyros Hallalu*, and *Maoz Tzur*. They relate the wonders which God performed for the Jews of long ago through Judah the Hasmonean and his brave band of Maccabees. This moment of remembrance around the light of a single candle is a proud one for the entire family.

At dinner the *Latke* makes its appearance for the first time during the week. It has a long and honorable history as the chief Hanukkah delicacy, and no wonder! Who can resist the pleasure of eating golden brown potato pancakes, crisp and hot?

An old custom connected with Hanukkah is playing games and the favorite game is the *dreydel*. A dreydel is a four-sided top on which the Hebrew letters *Nun* (N), *Gimel* (G), *Heh* (H) and *Shin* (Sh) are engraved. These stand for the Hebrew words *Nes Gadol Hayah Sham* which means *A Great Miracle Took Place There*. They also stand for the Yiddish-German words *Nem* (*take*), *Gib* (*give*), *Halb* (*half*) and *Shtel tzu* (*add*). The custom of spinning tops on Hanukkah originated in Germany. So to this day dreydels are made with directions for the game printed on them in a kind of code language in Yiddish.

Besides this well known form of the game, there are many variations. Many people like to spin the dreydel just for the sheer fun of it. But any way you play it, it's pleasant to while away a happy hour or two on Hanukkah night with a sturdy dreydel and a few good friends.

Hanukkah is of course a time for big family celebrations. Grandparents, uncles, aunts and cousins get together at least once during Hanukkah week. They light the candles, sing the blessings and the hymns and eat the festive meal. Then comes the time for Hanukkah gifts for the children. In some families the earlier tradition of giving Hanukkah Gelt, or Hanukkah money, is still followed. But whether *gelt* or gifts, everyone believes that this is a time for sharing joys and for giving gifts.

This then is the way Hanukkah is celebrated today. Families gather to enjoy the holiday. Mountains of latkes are eaten, the dreydel spins right through the week and there are gifts galore. And in every Jewish home candles burn for eight nights to remind us of the great miracle which took place *bayamim hahem bazman hazeh,* in those days, at this season. And everyone knows that Hanukkah has come again.

Hanukkah In Other Lands

The observance of Hanukkah varies little from country to country among Jews of the West, but in the East, among the Jews of North Africa and Asia, there are many unusual customs surrounding the Hanukkah festival. Here are descriptions of some of these customs.

Iranian Jews observe Hanukkah within the family circle. At home and in the synagogue they tell stories which celebrate the heroism of the Maccabees; each particular tale of valour is told and retold with great interest year in, year out.

The Hanukkah lamps of Iranian Jews are made of a metal, such as tin and come in nine separate sections. All year long they are stored away on a high shelf near the ceiling, and on the eve of Hanukkah they are brought out to be used for the festival.

The woman of the house spins wicks out of cotton, braids them and sets them into the lamps. Every day of the festival she cleans the lamps, removes the burned out wicks and replaces them with fresh ones. In the evening after prayers, the father lights the lamps. Frequently father and son alternate in the performance of the lamplighting, the father lighting the lamp on the first night, the son on the second night, then father and son again on the third and fourth nights until the end of the festival. In this way, it is believed, children will learn to perform the ceremony easily and naturally.

After the lamplighting the family sits down to its evening meal around a table covered with a heavy blanket. Those eating can stretch their legs under the blanket and be warmed by the fire of a brazier which has been lit under the table. No special foods are eaten on Hanukkah, nor are gifts of money distributed, except to the children of the poor who come knocking on the doors.

On Hanukkah nights groups of children go from house to house carrying a small stove alive with burning coal and a bagful of *aspenad*, a plant which pops when it is thrown into the fire. This is believed to be a magic charm against the evil eye. One of the children sings a folk ditty set to a droning eastern tune and the others chime in on a refrain after each stanza. When the song is ended the head of the house tosses the singers a small coin in return for which one of the children takes a handful of the *aspenad*, waves it toward the four corners of the house and then throws it into the burning coals. As it explodes noisily he cries, "So may your enemies perish!"

As on all festivals, on Hanukkah too the betrothed young man showers his bride-to-be with gifts and confections — preserves, pastries and small cakes decorated in gold paper. The father of the bride then invites the young man to a feast for friends and relatives of both families. They eat, drink, sing and make merry late into the night.

On the last night of Hanukkah the burned out wicks are gathered on the reverse side of a copper tray. The father lights them and recites the thirtieth psalm, the psalm which sings of the dedication of the House of David. He then throws into the burning tray roast peas, nuts and other such delicacies. The children scramble for them and eat their fill, and what they can't finish that night they share with their friends at school the next day.

In Antioch, Syria, the entire Jewish community orders candles from Jerusalem. When they arrive, everyone, young and old, goes to hail their arrival with songs of praise. The candles are then sold publicly in the synagogue and the profit is used for the support of the community religious school.

In Damascus, Syria, children are given Hanukkah candles instead of gifts. The teachers send each family a candle made in the form of a hand, that is, a palm with five upright fingers. This is meant to protect the children from an evil eye. On the day of the dedication of the altar, on the 25th day of Kislev, the children bring gifts to the chief rabbi of the city.

In Iraq on Hanukkah mothers bake poppyseed cookies, honey cakes and other sweet delicacies which the children bring to school. There, students and teachers feast upon them together.

In Morocco on Hanukkah young children are dressed in tradi- tional fringed garments and are given gifts of new prayerbooks so that they may learn the blessings for Hanukkah.

In Tunisia on Hanukkah the children bedeck their menorahs with flowers and receive as a reward handfuls of coins caller *flower money.*

In Bucharia on Hanukkah the custom is to send to teachers and to poor relatives cakes filled with coins of gold and silver.

In Yemen on Hanukkah the children make menorahs of clay for themselves. They then light their own candles and recite the blessings. The parents have their own menorahs and bless the candles separately.

In Israel, Hanukkah is a great public festival

For the people of Israel feel that the spirit of the Maccabees surrounds them everywhere. They believe that the Maccabean struggle for freedom was repeated only a few years ago on the same ancient soil. The name which the Israelis gave to the modern struggle is the War of Independence. It took place in 1948-49.

In that year this small and courageous people defended itself and its freedom against a more numerous and better armed enemy. And again the weak defeated the strong, the few defeated the many. Again the people of Israel overcame the encircling enemy which wanted to destroy it.

The miraculous quality of these twin victories, separated by two thousand years, has turned the observance of Hanukkah in Israel into a brilliant and impressive spectacle.

For eight days the whole country sparkles with lights. Giant menorahs blaze from the highest buildings in every large city, in each town and village. From the roof of the Knesset, Israel's Parliament building in Jerusalem, from the Great Synagogue in Tel Aviv, from the town halls in the Valley of Jezreel, from the hills of the Galilee and from the water towers of the Negev settlements, a chain of beacon lights shines forth and proclaims: *"This is the Feast of Hanukkah!"*

The most thrilling event in the week-long celebration is the great Freedom Torch Relay which welcomes the holiday to Israel. The Relay begins in Modin, the home of the Maccabees, which lies about twelve miles northwest of Jerusalem. A huge bonfire is lit and there the first runners kindle the torches which they bring in relays to the furthest corners of the country and back again to Jerusalem. On their way they pass through the large cities and through small scattered villages so that every Israeli may see the Torch of Freedom with his own eyes. When after a steep ascent through the Judean hills the runners reach Jerusalem, they are welcomed jubilantly by the President of the State of Israel and by the people of Jerusalem.

The Israelis believe the Freedom Torch Relay to be a reenactment of an ancient ascent to freedom. For it was to Jerusalem that Judah Maccabee came with his Freedom Fighters, there to rekindle the flame of liberty. And it is to Jerusalem now, as then, that Israeli youth bring lighted torches to rekindle the spirit of courage and to rededicate themselves to the ideal of freedom and independence.

The First Book of Maccabees

We know the accurate facts of the Hanukkah story today because more than 2000 years ago an anonymous historian wrote a vivid account of the Maccabean Revolt. That account is contained in the First Book of Maccabees.

Although the writer of the First Book of Maccabees is anonymous (his name is nowhere recorded), scholars know several things about him. They know that he lived during or soon after the Maccabean uprising. He wrote in the style of an on-the-spot reporter, as if he had been an eye witness to the events which he describes. They know further that he wrote his chronicles after victory had been won by the Jews, probably during the reign of one of the early Hasmonean kings who ruled independent Judea. Judging by his first hand knowledge of the facts it is even believed that he may have been court historian and that he had before him the court records of each battle and each phase of the struggle.

And finally it is clear that the author of the First Book of Maccabees was a loyal and enthusiastic patriot of the Kingdom of Judea—for he wrote with pride of the victorious deeds of the Hasmoneans and of the achievements of the Judean state.

The First Book of Maccabees was originally written in Hebrew in a style similar to the style of the Bible. But it is not and never was a part of the Hebrew Bible. It belongs to a group of writings known as *The Apocrypha* which is simply a Greek name for ancient books not included in the Bible. For there were many religious and historical books written in ancient times. But only the most important ones were included in the Bible.

The original Hebrew version of the First Book of Maccabees was lost. But fortunately it had first been translated into Greek and it was preserved in a Greek translation of the Bible known as the Septuagint. Scholars discovered in the Septuagint the facts of the wars between the Syrians and the Jews and were able to reconstruct a glorious period in Jewish history. We today read it and know it as the story of Hanukkah.

And so we see that books too have interesting lives. An ancient record lost in Hebrew was found in Greek and translated back into Hebrew, into English and into many other languages.

The adventure of the First Book of Maccabees is a thrilling one. It shows us that books have a life of their own. It teaches us that languages are bridges — between one people and another, between the past and the present. And most important it holds up a clear and accurate mirror to the past.

Here are some selections from the First Book of Maccabees. You will certainly recognize them as parts of the Hanukkah story you know so well.

*　　*　　*

... And after that Antiochus had smitten Egypt, he returned again in the hundred forty and third year, and went up against Israel and Jerusalem with a great multitude, and entered proudly into the sanctuary, and took away the golden altar and the candlestick of light and all the vessels thereof and the table of the showbread, and the pouring vessels, and the vials, and the censers of gold, and the veil, and the crowns, and the golden ornaments, that were before the temple. He took also the hidden treasures which he found. And when he had taken all away he went into his own land, having made a great massacre, and spoken very proudly. Therefore there was great mourning in Israel.

The Decree of Antiochus

Moreover, King Antiochus wrote to his whole kingdom that all should be one people, and every one should learn his laws; so all the heathen agreed according to the commandment of the King. Yea, many also of the Israelites consented to his religion, and sacrificed unto idols, and profaned the Sabbath. For the King had sent letters by messengers unto Jerusalem and the cities of Judah, that they should follow the strange laws of the land, and forbid burnt offerings, and sacrifice, and drink offerings in the temple; and that they should profane the Sabbaths and festival days, and pollute the sanctuary and them that were holy, and set up altars, and groves and chapels of idols, and sacrifice swine's flesh and unclean beasts, and that they should also leave their children uncircumcised, and make their souls abominable with all manner of uncleanness and profanation, to the end that they might forget the law and change all the ordinances. And whosoever would not do according to the commandment of the king, he said, he should die. In the selfsame manner wrote he to his whole kingdom, and appointed overseers over all the people, commanding the cities of Judah to sacrifice, city by city. Then many of the people were gathered unto them, to wit, every one that forsook the law; and so they committed evils in the land; and drove the Israelites into secret places, even wheresoever they could flee for succour.

Now on the fifteenth day of the month Kislev, in the hundred and fifty year, they set up the abomination of desolation upon the altar, and builded idol altars throughout the cities of Judah on every side; and burned incense at the doors of their houses, and in the streets. And when they had rent in pieces the books of the Law which they found, they burnt them with fire. And whosoever was found with any Book of the Covenant, or if any consented to the Law, the King's commandment was that they put him to death. Thus did they by their authority unto the Israelites every month, to as many as were found in the cities.

Now on the five and twentieth day of the month they did sacrifice upon the idol altar, which was upon the altar of God. At which time according to the commandment they put to death certain women, that had caused their children to be circumcised. And they hanged the infants about their necks, and rifled their houses, and slew them that had circumcised them. Howbeit many in Israel were fully resolved and confirmed in themselves not to eat any unclean thing. Wherefore they chose rather to die, that they might not be defiled with meats, and that they might not profane the holy covenant; so then they died. And there was very great wrath upon Israel.

The Heroism of Mattathias

In those days arose Mattathias, the son of John, the son of Simeon, a priest of the sons of Joarib, from Jerusalem, and dwelt in Modin. And he had five sons, John who was surnamed Gaddis; Simon called Thassi; Judas, who was called Maccabeus; Eleazer, called Avaran; and Jonathan, whose surname was Apphus.

In the meanwhile the King's officers, such as compelled the people to revolt, came into the city Modin to make them sacrifice. And when many of Israel came unto them, Mattathias also and his sons came together. Then answered the king's officers, and said to Mattathias on this wise: "Thou art a ruler and an honourable and great man in this city, and strengthened with sons and brethren. Now therefore come thou first, and fulfil the king's commandment, like as all the heathen have done, yea, and the men of Judah also, and such as remain at Jerusalem, so shalt thou and thy house be in the number of the king's friends, and thou and thy children shall be honoured with silver and gold, and many rewards." Then Mattathias answered and spake with a loud voice; "Though all the nations that are under the king's dominion obey him and fall away every one from the religion of their fathers, and give consent to his commandments, yet will I and my sons and my brethren walk in the covenant of our fathers. God forbid that we should forsake the law and the ordinances. We will not hearken to the king's words to go from our religion, either on the right hand or the left."

Now when he had left speaking these words there came one of the Jews in the sight of all to sacrifice on the altar which was at Modin, according to the king's commandment. Which thing when Mattathias saw, he was inflamed with zeal, and his reins trembled, neither could he forbear to show his anger according to judgment; wherefore he ran, and slew him upon the altar. Also the king's commissioner, who compelled men to sacrifice, he killed at that time, and the altar he pulled down. Thus dealt he zealously for the law of God, like as Phinehas did unto Zimri the son of Salu. And Mattathias cried throughout the city with a loud voice, saying: "Whosoever is zealous of the law and maintaineth the covenant, let him follow me." So he and his sons fled into the mountains, and left all that ever they had in the city.

The Death of Mattathias

Now when the time drew near that Mattathias should die, he said unto his sons: "Now hath pride and rebuke gotten strength, and the time of destruction, and the wrath of indignation. Now therefore, my sons, be ye zealous for the law, and give your lives for the covenant of your fathers . . . Be valiant, and show yourselves men in the behalf of the law; for by it shall ye obtain glory. And, behold, I know that your brother, Simon, is a man of counsel, give ear unto him always; he shall be a father unto you. As for Judas Maccabeus, he hath been mighty and strong, even from his youth up; let him be your captain, and fight the battle of the people. Take also unto you all those that observe the law, and avenge ye the wrong of your people. Recompense fully the heathen, and take heed to the commandments of the law."

So he blessed them, and was gathered to the fathers. And he died in the hundred forty and sixth year, and his sons buried him in the sepulchres of his father at Modin, and all Israel made great lamentation for him.

The Maccabee

Then his son Judah, called Maccabeus, rose up in his stead. And all his brethren helped him, and so did all they that held with his father, and they fought with cheerfulness the battle of Israel. So he got his people great honour, and put on a breastplate as a giant, and girt his warlike harness about him, and he made battles, protecting the host with his sword. In his acts he was like a lion, and like a lion's whelp roaring for his prey. For he pursued the wicked, and sought them out, and burnt out those that vexed his people. Wherefore the wicked shrank for fear of him, and all the workers of iniquity were troubled, because salvation prospered in his hand. He grieved also many kings, and made Jacob glad with his acts, and his memorial is blessed for ever. Moreover he went through the cities of Judah, destroying the ungodly out of them and turning away wrath from Israel; so that he was renowned into the utmost part of the earth, and he received unto him such as were ready to perish.

Victory over Lysias

In the next year Lysias gathered together threescore thousand choice men of foot, and five thousand horsemen, that he might subdue them. So they came into Idumaea and pitched their tents at Bethsura, and Judah met them with ten thousand men.

So they joined battle; and there were slain of the host of Lysias about five thousand men, even before them were they slain.

Now when Lysias saw his army put to flight, and the manliness of Judah's soldiers and how they were ready either to live or die valiantly, he went to Antiochia and gathered together hired soldiers, and having made his army greater than it was, he purposed to come again into Judea.

Then said Judah and his brethren: "Behold, our enemies are discomfited; let us go up to cleanse and dedicate the sanctuary."

The Dedication of the Sanctuary

Now on the five and twentieth day of the ninth month, which is called the month of Kislev, in the hundred forty and eighth year, they rose up betimes in the morning, and offered sacrifice according to the law upon the new altar of burnt offerings, which they had made. Look, at what time and what day the heathen had profaned, even in that was it dedicated with songs, and citherns, and harps, and cymbals. Then all the people fell upon their faces, worshipping and praising the God of heaven, who had given them good success. And so they kept the dedication of the altar eight days, and offered burnt offerings with gladness and sacrificed the sacrifice of deliverance and praise. They decked also the forefront of the temple with crowns of gold and with shields; and the gates and the chambers they renewed, and hanged doors upon them.

Thus was there very great gladness among the people, for that the reproach of the heathen was put away. Moreover Judah and his brethren with the whole congregation of Israel ordained that the days of the dedication of the altar should be kept from year to year by the space of eight days, from the five and twentieth day of the month of Kislev, with mirth and gladness.

Jewish tradition has handed down some simple suggestions for the observance of Hanukkah. These reflect the special love of Jews for this festival of miracles and their desire to make it a beautiful and memorable festival for the entire family.

At nightfall all members of the family should gather around the menorah to participate in the candlelighting. To enhance the beauty of the ceremony there are even specific directions about the order and the manner of the ritual. For example, we are told that on the first evening of Hanukkah one candle is lit, on the second evening two are kindled, and each night another is added until the eighth night when all eight candles are lit. We are further guided by tradition which tells us to place the first candle at the right end of the menorah and to add each new one from the left. As for the direction of the lighting, the tradition provides for that too. The newly added candles must always be lit first and then the lighting proceeds from left to right.

And what about the candles and the menorahs, has Jewish tradition anything to say about these? It does indeed! It tells us that all the candles must be of equal height, with the exception of the *shamash*, the servant candle, which is slightly higher than the others. These should be placed in a straight row with enough space between them so that they do not stick together or drip and so spoil the beauty of the menorah.

And finally, the Hanukkah candles should be large enough to burn for at least thirty minutes. Moreover, they should be set into a menorah of metal or of silver, as beautiful and as precious a menorah as possible, so that each night as long as the candles burn, their radiance may be reflected in the menorah which holds them.

There were probably many questions in ancient times about Hanukkah. What kind of festival is it? What is permitted and what is not permitted on Hanukkah? In answer to such questions the rabbis of old decided that all manner of work is permitted during the entire week of the holiday except while the candles are burning each night. They ruled too that on Friday night the Hanukkah candles must be lit before the Sabbath candles, so that the sacredness of the Sabbath should not be disturbed.

Because Hanukkah celebrates a great and miraculous victory, Jews, out of a deep sense of gratitude, recite psalms of praise and thanksgiving each morning of Hanukkah. These psalms are known as the "Hallel" prayer. Wishing to include the entire family in the circle of thanksgiving, Jewish tradition believes that women and older children too should light the menorah, because in ancient times women and children, as much as men, benefited from the miracle and the glory of Hanukkah.

Legends About Hanukkah

Legend and history are inseparable!

Any person who has left his mark upon time and any event which has influenced the course of history are surrounded by legend. Because facts alone do not satisfy people's desire for knowledge about the past. People want to know the whole story. They ask: "What else was there?" "What more happened?"

Then, out of the shadows of the past, stories are remembered and tales are told, some factual and some imagined. And so slowly a legend is born. Time nourishes a legend and helps it grow. Unseen, time slips in and gradually erases the boundary line between fact and fancy until they become inseparable. And then when people ask "Is it true?" we can only say — "Perhaps — we don't really know — but it could be true."

The important question about a legend is not "Is it true?" but rather, "What truth does it tell us?" For odd as it may seem, a legend is often more true than actual historical facts.

History tells us how people lived in the past and what they did.

Legend reveals what people believed and hoped and dreamed. Legends are in a way the collective dreams of many people taken from the slumbering past and told as stories.

Legends do even more. They inspire with their stories of heroism and greatness. They teach the lessons which are stored up in the wisdom of the past.

We have already discovered that the First Book of Maccabees is an important historical record. The Second Book of Maccabees is important too. It is a collection of inspiring legends concerning Hanukkah. We have chosen some of these, and others too, from other books because they tell us what the people of ancient Judea hoped and believed. We have chosen them because they inspire and teach important truths out of the past.

Hannah and Her Seven Sons

In the days when Antiochus was King of Syria there lived a woman named Hannah who had seven sons. Mother and sons were thrown into prison where they were cruelly tortured because they refused to eat forbidden food. One of them spoke for the rest and said, "We are ready to die rather than break the laws of our fathers."

At these words the King flew into a mad rage and commanded that he be put to death by terrible tortures before the eyes of his mother and brothers. And so it was. They brought the young man forward and began to work their barbarous torments upon him. His mother and brothers witnessed this dread sight and strengthened one another, saying, "The Lord watches over us in our suffering and takes joy in our steadfastness."

The merciless tyrant, seeing the first son die so courageously, ordered that the next son be brought forward and decreed that the same savage tortures be inflicted upon him. And on the third son. And on the fourth and the fifth and the sixth.

Each died nobly and fearlessly, neither shrinking from the cruelties of the Syrians nor crying out in protest, but trusting in God as he breathed his last. The heartless King and his soldiers marvelled at the brothers' courage for they totally disregarded all pain.

But above all the mother was marvelous in her fortitude. For when she saw her seven sons killed in one day she bore it all bravely and with deep faith in the Lord.

While the youngest son was still alive Antiochus decided to appeal to him with temptations of riches and honor. The king promised to make the lad his friend if only he would forsake the faith of his fathers. But the boy would not listen. So Antiochus turned to the mother and urged her to prevail upon her only remaining son to save himself by yielding to the King's wishes. This she mockingly agreed to do. But instead she spoke to him in this manner.

"My son, have pity upon your mother who bore you and nourished you and raised you to this age. I beg you, fear not this base murderer. Prove yourself worthy of your brothers and choose death!"

To this he replied, "I will not obey the King's commandment, but only the commandment of the law that was given to our fathers by Moses. Like my brothers, I give up my body and soul for that law."

The King, seeing that he had been mocked, became enraged, and treated him more barbarously than the rest.

And so the boy died, putting his whole trust in the Lord.

And last of all, after her sons, the mother died.

A Menorah of Spears

An old legend provides a second explanation for the custom of kindling lights for eight nights at Hanukkah.

When the victorious Maccabees entered the Temple to cleanse it of the defilement of the heathens, they looked for the menorah of gold, one of the holy vessels of the Temple. But it was nowhere to be found, for Antiochus had taken it for himself. Instead of a menorah the Maccabees found eight spears of iron at the altar. On each of these they placed a bowl of oil and they kindled the lights. They kindled the lights of this crude menorah for eight days and for eight days the spears of the Syrians brought light and joy and gladness to the Jews.

Judith and Holofernes

In his great greed Antiochus wanted to conquer the whole world. So he sent his most famous general, Holofernes, to subdue the lands of the east. With an impressive army Holofernes marched from one country to another; he sacked countless cities, dispersed the people and destroyed their temples.

After twelve years Holofernes came to Jerusalem determined to destroy its fortress and its holy temple. Akior, a captive king from one of the lands of the east, warned the arrogant general:

"Do not molest these people and do not encircle their holy city, for their God is with them. He will not deliver them into your hands but will avenge Himself upon anyone who desires to harm them."

But Holofernes refused to listen and marched upon Jerusalem. When the people of Jerusalem learned that a mighty army was approaching, they strengthened their army, fortified the city and guarded all the mountain passes leading to its main gate.

Holofernes arrived at the foot of the hills surrounding the holy city. Outside the city gates he discovered the wells and the springs which supplied water to the inhabitants of Jerusalem. He immediately took possession of these, for he thought, "Why should I fight the Jews with swords and spears? I will deprive them of their water supply. They will weaken and die of thirst. Then Jerusalem will be mine without a battle."

It soon appeared that Holofernes' plan would succeed. Twenty days after the onset of the siege, all of Jerusalem's cisterns were dry. The situation was dangerously critical. Women and children languished for lack of water. The weak and the faint lay on the roads and the dead increased in the gates of the city.

The people, desperate by now, confronted their two chief leaders, Uzziah and Carmi, and cried out: "We can endure this thirst no longer. Let us seek relief! Let us surrender to the enemy!"

Uzziah and Carmi, seeing that their distress was great, pleaded with them:

"Let us wait five more days. Perhaps God in His mercy will send us salvation. If in five days there is no other way we will surrender."

Now there lived in Jerusalem a wealthy widow named Judith who was pious and wise and exceedingly beautiful. Since her husband's death, three years before, she dressed in sackcloth and spent her time in a crude lean-to near her palatial home grieving for her husband. When Judith learned that Jerusalem might be forced to surrender to the Syrians in five days' time, she sent to Uzziah and Carmi and said to them:

"My brothers, the situation in Jerusalem is desperate, but we dare not surrender, for exile and desolateness are worse than death itself. I have a plan which may save our people and our beloved city."

The elders listened eagerly as Judith continued:

"Tonight my hand-maiden and I will leave the city. Let no man ask us where we go or for what purpose, for I can divulge nothing until the thing which I plan is done."

To this Uzziah and Carmi agreed, saying:

"Go in peace and may God crown your mission with success."

At dusk Judith knelt in prayer before the Lord and asked for wisdom and strength for the sake of her people. Then she dressed herself in her loveliest garments and adorned herself with the costliest jewels, for her intention was to dazzle Holofernes. To her hand-

maiden she gave flasks of milk, skins of wine, oil, flour, bread and cheese to carry. Thus prepared they silently left the city in the dark of night.

Syrian sentries discovered them at dawn as they were making their way down the mountain paths, and took them to Holofernes' tent. The rays of the rising sun streaked the sky with crimson spokes when Holofernes beheld Judith for the first time. From that moment he was bewitched by her extraordinary beauty. Gently he asked her what she, a Jewess, was doing in the Syrian camp, and Judith replied:

"Your victory, O Holofernes, is a certainty, for our God has abandoned His people because of their wickedness. I have come to lead your men to Jerusalem through hidden ways and secret clefts in the rocks. Our God appeared to me in a vision and bade me tell you that the people of Jerusalem will not withstand your might."

With these words Judith captivated Holofernes completely. "Not only is this woman beautiful," thought he, "but her understanding cannot be surpassed among women." He welcomed her to his camp and ordered that she and her hand-maiden be installed in an elegant tent befitting so noble a lady. Before accepting his hospitality Judith said:

"There are two things which I ask of you my lord. You must allow me and my hand-maiden to eat of the foods which we brought with us. Whatever must be, must be, but I am a Jewess and I serve my God in all ways. Your food is forbidden me."

To this Holofernes readily agreed.

"The other thing which I desire is that my hand-maiden and I be permitted to pray to our God each evening outside the camp, unseen by anyone, for such was our custom always. In this way God will reveal to me when it is time to attack Jerusalem."

To this too Holofernes agreed, for by now he was hopelessly enamored of Judith.

For three days Judith lived among the Syrian soldiers. Each evening she and her hand-maiden left the camp unhindered and went into the fields to pray. With their faces turned toward Jerusalem they asked for God's blessing. They then returned to the camp and to their tent.

At the end of the third day Holofernes made a great feast to which he invited Judith. She graciously agreed to come. Her hand-maiden went before her and spread soft skins for her mistress at the foot of Holofernes' chair. She also brought food and wine from her tent, a plate of silver and a goblet for the wine.

Then Judith arrived and she was radiantly beautiful.

They began to feast and to drink and to make merry with abandon. Judith offered Holofernes some cheese which she had brought from Jerusalem. He ate with great relish until his thirst knew no bounds. So Judith poured him cup after cup of wine until he became drowsy. By now everyone had left, for the night was half over and all were tired from the carousing. Only Judith remained with Holofernes, who soon fell into a sound drunken sleep.

While her hand-maiden stood guard at the door, Judith unsheathed the shining sword which hung above his canopied bed and with one sharp stroke she cut off his head. Then she and her hand-maiden slipped out of the camp unmolested, for the guards had become accustomed to their nightly walks into the hills and no one suspected mischief in the camp.

They quickly made their way over the hills to Jerusalem. There Judith proclaimed to a grateful city that the enemy general had been struck down. Hearing this, the people of Jerusalem armed themselves and streamed down the mountains toward the enemy camp. The Syrian sentries, sighting them from a distance, sent word to Holofernes that the Jews were approaching, armed, and in fighting spirit.

But Holofernes had been beheaded! No sooner was word of his death out when terror seized the Syrian armies. They fled wildly in every direction, abandoning their wealth, their weapons and their supplies. The Jews pursued them and totally defeated them.

On that day might was turned to naught, glory to death and the weak set the strong to flight. This God chose to do through Judith, a beautiful and fearless woman of Jerusalem. The memory of her courageous deed lives on for generations.

Why Jews Spin the Dreydel

An old legend relates how the Hanukkah dreydel was invented during the time of the Maccabees.

Antiochus the Syrian tyrant forbade our ancestors to study the Torah or to gather in a synagogue. But the Jews would not forsake the Torah. So they met secretly in small groups and in hidden places and studied the Torah by heart. In that way if one forgot a passage, another who remembered could teach it to him while a third person served as lookout at the door. When soldiers approached, a warning was given and the group would quickly break up and disappear through back doors and secret passages.

One of the tricks that were used to avoid discovery was the dreydel game. This is how it was done. The students always kept a top on the table while they were studying. If a soldier appeared before the members of the group could melt away, one of them would begin to spin the dreydel and all would pretend enthusiastically that they were engaging in an innocent game. The soldier had no way of proving otherwise. And so, a little Hanukkah dreydel saved the lives of many loyal and pious Jews.

The Children of the Maccabees

Jedayah was a descendant of the noble priestly family of Simon the Just. He was among the oldest and most esteemed of the priests of Jerusalem. He would have been altogether content but for the fact that he had no children. And this was a great sorrow to the gentle old man.

Day and night Jedayah prayed to God that He might bless him with a son to carry on the traditions of the illustrious family of Simon the Just. One night, as he was praying in the Temple, the glad word came to him that God would grant him his wish. A voice called, "Jedayah! Jedayah! Know that a son shall indeed be born to thee. Call thou his name Peli. But on the day that he enters the world thou shalt leave it!"

At the same season the following year, the wife of Jedayah bore him a son; and they called him Peli.

And, as had been foretold, on the day that Peli was born, his father died.

Peli was a beautiful child with dark shining eyes and a gentle, musical voice. Whoever saw him loved him immediately. When Peli opened his eyes for the first time and saw the great heavenly lights and the beautiful carpet of flowers that covered the earth he cried out ecstatically, "Hallelujah!"

It therefore came about that he was known as *Hallelujah*, even though his given name was Peli.

As the boy grew up, he had the ablest and most learned teachers in Jerusalem; and, as time went on he became known as one of the wisest children of Jerusalem.

Hallelujah would often wander beyond the city to climb the steep hills on the outskirts of Jerusalem. There he would gaze at the clear blue sky above him and at the quiet waters of Shiloh flowing below. His eyes would gleam with a strange joy, and he would whisper, quietly to himself, "Hallelujah! Hallelujah!"

Later, on his way home through the streets of the city, he would pass the splendid Temple and again his rosy little lips would form the glad word, "Hallelujah!" But his real name was Peli.

Then there came dreadful days upon Israel. Syrian soldiers entered Jerusalem by the thousands, profaned the Holy Temple, slew women and children without mercy, tortured the wise men. The streets of Jerusalem ran red with the blood of the innocent and the zealous. Many escaped and hid themselves in caves but were found by the Syrian soldiers and brutally massacred.

Close to the Mount of Olives, east of Jerusalem, there was a deep secret cave. There several hundred children fled for their lives. They wept bitterly and prayed for their loved ones, who had fallen by the sword of the cruel enemy.

From among them a boy arose and addressed them all. "Harken, ye children of Jerusalem!"

"Peace! Peace! *Hallelujah* speaks!" the word flashed around the cave.

Hundreds of innocent young eyes turned toward the speaker.

Hallelujah's melodious, inspiring young voice rang out:

"Children of Jerusalem! Weep not for the heroes who have died the deaths of martyrs! Weep rather for us, the living, who must see our Holy City desolate, our Sanctuary profaned by the heathen! Weep for us, the young and the weak. Who knows whether we will be permitted to live, or whether we too, will die for our country and for our God — who knows?"

There was no word heard in answer, only sobbing and sighing.

And the sweet voice of Hallelujah became stronger and more resolute. "And we — are we not children of Jerusalem? Comrades, let us swear! Let us swear, by the souls of our martyred parents, by the Scroll of the Law itself, that we shall live for our people, our country and our God, if we may, and die for them, if we must!"

"We swear! We swear!" shouted the children, in chorus.

They were interrupted by the clanking of swords at the mouth of the cave. A band of Syrian soldiers had approached.

"Come out, children," shouted the leader." "We shall not harm you!"

The eyes of all the children were turned toward their little spokesman.

"Will you keep your oath?" he questioned.

31

"That we will! Never fear!" shouted the children in answer.

"Come out, children! We will not kill you," came the leader's second call.

Not a sound came from the children inside. Then from the mouth of the cave great, dark clouds of smoke came floating toward the children. A fire had been lit — the flames spread quickly carrying the choking fumes deeper and deeper into the cave.

"Children of Jerusalem! Let us all die together for our own people and for our God!" *Hallelujah's* voice rang out clearer and stronger than before.

"For our people and our God!" echoed the children.

The cave became intolerably hot and stifling.

"Shema Yisroel!" prayed *Hallelujah*, above the din.

"Hear, O Israel! The Lord our God, the Lord is One!" answered the children, falling into each others arms.

Suddenly, a door opened in the side of the cave (no one had ever known that there was such a door) and an old man with a long white beard, wearing the priestly robes of white, stood before them. It was Jedayah, the father of *Hallelujah*.

"Beloved children," he said in a kind and fatherly voice. "You will not die. Have no fear. You will live to fight the battles of God and of Israel."

The children looked about them and saw that they were now in a vast field, with many great trees and beautiful flowers. Birds more gorgeous than any they had ever seen flew about among the branches, and sang with heavenly sweetness, "Hallelujah! Hallelujah!"

"Now," said their aged savior, "go forward, my children, go forward and redeem your unhappy people and your desolate land! March forward, and my son shall lead you to victory!"

And the birds sang "Hallelujah" as though it were a refrain to the old priest's words.

But the children shouted, "Hedad! (Hurrah) Hallelujah!"

The wonderful old man vanished as suddenly as he had come, and the field and the trees and flowers and birds disappeared with him. Instead close by lay the town of Modin, the home of the heroic Maccabees, where their army lay encamped.

The next day, Captain Judah set the young band in the forefront of the battle with the enemy. Crying "Hallelujah!" the children fell upon them. When the Syrians saw this, they trembled and shook with terror, saying to one another, "Surely these are the souls of the Hebrew children whom we slew." So terrorized were they, that they scattered in every direction. The Jewish army followed them in hot pursuit, and put many of them to the sword.

When Judah Maccabeus finally led his victorious patriots into Jerusalem to dedicate the Temple, Hallelujah and his brigade proudly headed the brave soldiers.

That is why Jewish children celebrate the Hanukkah festival with exultation and rejoicing. They know that just as their ancestors resisted the enemies of Israel, so they too have the privilege of serving their people and their faith.

Blood of the Maccabees

On the morning after Judah Maccabee was slain in battle, lovely white flowers flecked with blood-red dots sprouted on the battle field. People called these blossoms "Blood of the Maccabees." To this very day they grow in the hills of Judea covering the mountainsides with beautiful clusters of red and white which are startling to behold.

Each year at Hanukkah, children in Israel climb the hills to pick flowers for their holiday celebrations. Among the flowers they seek are the Blood of the Maccabees, the red-and-white symbols of the courage of Judah Maccabee.

The Miracle of the Jug of Oil

When the Syrian soldiers entered the Temple they defiled all the pure olive oil which the priests used to light the menorah.

Three years later the Maccabean victors marched into Jerusalem. They cleansed the Temple of its defilements and prepared to rededicate it to the service of the Lord. Finally everything was ready for the celebration of the Feast of Rededication. But when the time came to light the menorah, the seven-branched golden candlestick, there was no pure oil to be found anywhere throughout the Temple precincts.

Then in some hidden corner a little jug was found, tightly sealed with the seal of the High Priest. It contained just enough oil to burn for one day. The menorah was lit and the service of rededication was held. And the hearts of the people were full of gratitude and joy!

Then a miracle occurred!

For the little jugful of oil which was enough for only one day continued to burn for eight full days.

And so, to commemorate this miracle, Jews have observed the Feast of Lights from that time to this very day. The name they have given it is Hanukkah.

Poems for Hanukkah

Poems are to words what birthdays are to the days of the year.

At a birthday celebration we set our feelings free. We express feelings which we don't chatter about day by day. They are too precious and too important. We express them in a special language, with flowers and gifts, with a cake and candles, with a holiday feast!

A poem is a holiday feast of words. It may talk of a great and noble idea, of a vision of beauty or justice, of a feeling that runs deep and strong. It is written in language which is beautiful and free.

What do Hanukkah poems talk about?

About ideas that everyone can understand.

About feelings that everyone has felt.

About freedom and a people's struggle to achieve it.

About war and peace and the sweet taste of victory.

About anger and pride and fear and faith.

And about courage.

For these reasons and for others which you will probably discover for yourselves, these poems are suggested for your Hanukkah reading.

Judas The Maccabee

So he got his people great honour
And put on a breastplate as a giant,
And girt his warlike harness about him.
He fought battles,
Protecting the host with his sword.
In his acts he was like a lion,
Like a lion's whelp roaring for prey.
He pursued the wicked and sought them out;
He burned up those that vexed his people.
The wicked shrunk for fear of him,
The workers of iniquity were troubled,
Because victory was with him.
He grieved many kings,
He made Jacob glad,
His memory is blessed for ever.
He went through the cities of Judah
Destroying the ungodly,
Turning away wrath from Israel.
He was renowned to the ends of the earth.

—*First Book of Maccabees, Chapter 3*

Mattathias

He struck the traitor to the earth,
    He raised his sword that all might see;
His words rang like a trumpet blast:
    "All who are faithful, follow me!"
From near and far all Israel came:
    They rallied to his battle cry;
They prayed unto the God of Peace,
    And for their Lord went forth to die—
To die—and yet today they live;
    Far down the centuries flaming see
That beacon-sword! Hear that strong cry:
    "All who are faithful, follow me!"

—*Elma Ehrlich Levinger*

Judas Maccabeus to His Soldiers

O brothers, who have laid aside
  The ploughshare for the sword,
Who gather from the hills and plains
  To battle for the Lord:
If ye have hopes of honor,
  Or to reap wealth are fain,
Serve not the cause of Israel,
  But seek your homes again.

I have no golden gifts to give,
  Our land is stripped and bare;
Nor Grecian gauds and raiment rich—
  Behold the rags I wear!
They sleep on ivory couches,
  The rocks must be your bed;
Their tables groan with plenty,
  My men eat bitter bread.

No glories crown my faithful men,
  Who know the traitor's shame,
Until they meet in Syrian courts
  The death I dare not name.
My fighting hands are empty;
  My promises are grim;
Yet ye who honor Israel's God
  Will pledge your swords to Him.

—Elma Ehrlich Levinger

Hannah in the Dungeon

Be strong, my heart!
Break not till they are dead,
All, all my seven sons; then burst asunder
And let this tortured and tormented soul
Leap and rush out like water through the shards
Of earthen vessels broken at a well.
O my dear children, mine in life and death,
I neither gave you breath, nor gave you life.
And neither was it I that formed the members
Of every one of you. But the Creator,
Who made the world, and made the heavens above us,
Who formed the generations of mankind,
And found out the beginning of all things;
He gave you breath and life; and will again
Of his own mercy, as ye now regard
Not your own selves, but His eternal law.
I do not murmur, nay, I thank Thee, God,
That I and mine have not been deemed unworthy
To suffer for Thy sake, and for Thy law,
And for the many sins of Israel.
Hark! I can hear within the sound of scourges!
I feel them more than ye do, O my sons!
But cannot come to you. I, who was wont
To wake at night at the least cry ye made,
To whom ye ran at every slightest hurt,—
I cannot take you now into my lap
And soothe your pain, but God will take you all
Into his pitying arms, and comfort you,
And give you rest.

(*From the play, "Judas Maccabaeus"*)

—Henry W. Longfellow

Hasmonean Lights

Pure is the oil I take
My festal lights to kindle,
Lights of holiness,
Tiny lights,
Lights of God,
Reminders.
Of the miracle of the Hasmoneans.

Rage winds,
Fall snows,
My wicks are aflame!
Away, evil winds,
A drop of oil remains—
My lamp still burns—
Lights of God,
Lights of the Hasmoneans.

—*J. Fichman*

Blessings for Hanukkah

Blessed art Thou, O God our Lord,
Who made us holy with His word,
And told us on this feast of light
To light one candle more each night.

(Because when foes about us pressed
    To crush us all with death or shame,
The Lord His priests with courage blest
To strike and give His people rest
And in the House that He loved best
    Relit our everlasting flame.)

Blest art Thou, the whole world's King,
Who did so wonderful a thing
For our own fathers true and bold
At this same time in days of old!

—*Jessie E. Sampter*

My Hanukkah Candles

Eight little candles,
   All in a line;
Eight little candles
   Glitter and shine.

Eight little candles—
   Each little flame,
Whispers a legend
   Of honor and fame.

Eight little candles
   Bashfully hide
The soul of a people,
   Its hope and its pride . . .

Eight little candles,
   Sparklets of gold,
Stories of battles,
   And heroes of old.

Heroes undaunted,
   And noble and true;
Heroes who knew
   How to dare and to do;

Heroes who taught
  The ages to be
That man can be brave,
And that man should be free . . .

Eight little candles,
    Look at them well,
Floods could not quench them,
    Tempests not quell.

Modest and frail
    Is their light—yet it cheers
A people in exile
    Two thousand years . . .

Eight little candles—
    Their guttering gleams
Speak to my heart
    In a language of dreams.

Light to my eye
    Is their smile and their cheer,
Sweet to my ear
    Is their whisper to hear.

"Courage, but courage,
    Maccabee's brave son,
Fight for light—
    And the battle is won."

—*Philip M. Raskin*

Hail the Maccabees

Hear Judea's mountains ringing,
  Hail the Maccabees!
Hosts from cleft and cave upspringing,
  Hail the Maccabees!
Shining shields and spear-heads glancing,
See the lion brood advancing.
  Hail the Maccabees!
  Hail the Maccabees!

Wild the battle din is beating,
  Hail the Maccabees!
See the tyrant hordes retreating,
  Hail the Maccabees!
Loud shall rave the tyrant-weakling,
Mad Antiochus, the Greekling,
  Hail the Maccabees!
  Hail the Maccabees!

See the bright procession wending,
  Hail the Maccabees!
Hear the songs of praise ascending,
  Hail the Maccabees!
Holy—great the dedication
Of a liberated nation:
  Hail the Maccabees!
  Hail the Maccabees!

—Rufus Learsi

Before the Menorah

In the candle's rays I see
Lovely pictures beckoning me:
Judas with his shield and sword,
Pledged to battle for the Lord;
Eleazar, steadfast, strong,
'Mid the mocking heathen throng;
Hannah straight as candle's flame,
Sons who glorified her name—
Soldiers all, they smiled in pride,
Glad and unafraid they died—
God of Israel, may I be,
A soldier worthy of them and Thee!

—*Elma Ehrlich Levinger*

Hanukkah Oddities

Before every battle, Judah commanded that all those among his men who were building houses, planting vineyards, had just been married, or were afraid, should go home. This was required by Jewish law.

Hanukkah Lights the World Over

The kindling of Hanukkah lights was prohibited in the third century in Persia because the fire worshipping magicians, to whom fire was sacred, were in power.

In ancient times two great rabbis, Hillel and Shammai, had different opinions on how to light the Hanukkah candles. Shammai said that eight candles should be lit on the first night, and decreased by one each night. Hillel said that one candle should be lit on the first night and increased by one each night. Hillel's opinion prevailed and today we follow his method in lighting the Hanukkah candles.

In the synagogues in Algeria, the Hanukkah candles are lit in the morning instead of in the evening.

In the Caucasus the son kindles the lights and not the father.

Because the Menorah in the Temple was lit with oil, some people to this day prefer to use oil instead of candles to kindle their Hanukkah lights.

The Palestinian plant from which the candelabrum shaped menorah was probably taken is the seven-branched salvia plant.

The first day of Hanukkah can never occur on a Tuesday.

In olden times Jews placed Hanukkah candles outside the front door, and in Venice the Jews would row in gondolas through the ghetto and greet each house which had Hanukkah lights with songs and blessings.

Bible Readings On Hanukkah

Psalms of Thanksgiving (the Hallel prayers) are recited every morning throughout the eight days of Hanukkah.

Some scholars say that we began the custom of Haftorah (Prophets) reading when Antiochus forbade the Jews to read the Torah. He did not forbid them reading from the Prophets. Each

Haftorah was chosen because it was related in theme or idea to the Sidrah of the week. Thus the Haftorah helped the Jews remember the weekly Torah reading.

A portion of the Torah is read in the synagogue every morning during the week of Hanukkah.

Inspired by the Hanukkah Story

The famous composer Handel wrote an oratorio called "Judas Maccabeus" based on the story of Judah Maccabee.

The famous American poet, Henry Wadsworth Longfellow, wrcte a play in verse, called "Judas Maccabeus." It tells about the war with Antiochus, and the heroes of the Hanukkah story.

The famous Ma-oz Tzur song sung after kindling the Hanukkah lights was written by a poet named Mordecai in either the eleventh or the thirteenth century. The first letters of each stanza in Hebrew form his name. The fifth stanza tells the whole Hanukkah story in twenty-four Hebrew words.

Coins of the Maccabean Era

Antiochus used elephants against the Jewish warriors and one of the Maccabean coins has this animal engraved on it.

The British Museum in London contains the world's largest collection of ancient Maccabean coins.

The first official postage stamps issued by the new State of Israel in 1948 have a picture of the ancient Hasmonean coins of independence.

Origin of the Name

The name Maccabee comes from the first letters of the Hebrew prayer *Mi Kamocha Ba-elim Adonai* (Who is like unto Thee, O Lord!) inscribed on the Maccabean battle banner.

Another reason that Judah was called the Maccabee is that he struck with the force of a mighty hammer. The Hebrew word for hammer is Makav. Judah became known as "The Hammer" — or the Maccabee.

Simon Maccabee built a magnificent monument over his family's grave as Modin, which he surrounded by seven pyramids, as a memorial to his father, mother and four brothers and for himself when the time should come.

In 1918 General Allenby led the victorious Allied forces into Jerusalem on the 25th day of Kislev, which is the first night of Hanukkah.

Stories for Hanukkah

Ever since the world began and man first learned to use words, the story-teller and his craft have played an important role in communicating ideas and values. For thousands of years skillful story-tellers have been delighting their listeners with good tales well told, tales of action, tales of passion, tales with a moral, and above all tales that are exciting and entertaining.

Because, no matter where or in what language, people the world over have always enjoyed a good story.

In ancient times, in the orient, wise men sat in the gates of the city, or under the branches of a sacred tree, and passed on the wisdom of the tribe to those who sat at their feet. They told myths of the beginnings of their race, legends of tribal heroes, and folk tales of long, long ago when the world was young.

In the courts of the kings of Europe and Asia, after a day at the hunt and after a night of feasting, the lords and ladies would linger over their wine. Then bards were brought into the great halls and were asked to recite heroic accounts of war and adventure to entertain their royal hosts and the highborn guests.

Shahrazad, the heroine of the famous cycle of tales known as the Thousand and One Nights, fascinated Shahyaman, the King of India and China, by telling him the most marvelous tales ever heard by any king, a thousand and one in all. Through her skill as a story-teller she charmed the king and saved the lives of all the maidens of the realm.

To the best of our knowledge, the Hanukkah stories which follow have not been used to charm a king, although we believe that they certainly could. But of two things we have no doubt: That each of them carries a kernel or more of wisdom and that each of them is highly entertaining.

Read them, and judge for yourselves!

A Hanukkah Night in Old Philadelphia

(A Glimpse of Jewish Life in Revolutionary Days)
Leon Spitz

"And this will be the first time we shall ever have celebrated Hanukkah in our good city of Philadelphia."

The speaker was Manuel Josephson, the go-getter shopkeeper and Parness of the little Mikvah Israel Congregation in the year 1779. His voice rang with a joyous elation. He had been reared by his pious and learned father with a zeal for the faith of his people that few of his fellow Jewish merchants cared to emulate. No, they were much more interested in the mercantile clubs of the city — in the colonial politics — their sons and daughters eagerly sought admission into the fashionable City Dancing Assembly. They left the "minyan" to the impetuous Josephson, whose late father had bent too heavily over the folios of the Talmud to achieve commercial success and social prestige — even though he had certainly come of a good family — even a prominent family — over there in London.

That Josephson was really irrepressible. There was no stopping him and his overzealous interest in the projected synagogue. These were wartimes. The project could very well await a more propitious time.

But not Mr. Josephson. He had invited a full score of men and women, Philadelphians and even several of the southern refugees, to wit, that tall dignified looking old gentleman, a Mr. d'Acosta from Charleston in South Carolina — and — aha — there was Haym Salomon sitting at his ease, the youthful Polish New Yorker, who had recently broken away from a British prison-ship and had stealthily plodded his way into the city; there were others, really strangers, you understand — and some were revolutionary fire-brands. But Josephson had pooh-poohed all objections. They were Jews, weren't they! "Kol Yisroel chaverim." he quoted from his Talmud."All Jews are brothers and we are here for a Jewish cause." Nevertheless, it was quite an embarrassing situation; still, to argue over it would not mend matters.

So here they were, the leading Jews of Old Philadelphia, with their wives and spinster daughters, partaking of a wholesome kosher repast and regaling themselves with mellow wines. But in their hearts they entertained misgivings.

"Hanukkah, Hanukkah," muttered Mr. Levy, a partner to Mr. Franks in the well-known counting house which had carried through many a financial transaction for Lord Howe's army several months before, and were therefore suspect Tories and belonged to the city's blue-blooded aristocracy. "Ah, yea, that's all child stuff, a children's holiday. I recall faintly, candy, lights . . ."

But Rebecca Gratz, a slip of a girl, who sat so demurely between her two brothers, Michael and Bernard, was aroused to protest.

"Hanukkah is a festival of loyalty to Judaism. Moreover, it is a festival of high courage and patriotism — such as our people are displaying in our own American Struggle."

Rebecca Franks, well known in the city as a spirited Tory and toasted by the red-coat officers as the Belle of Philadelphia, sneered at her.

"Americans! Whom do you refer to, the redskin savages or perchance the Yankee Doodles?"

"Hush, my dear," her father cautioned her. "It is not wise to utter Tory sentiments so publicly, even though we are here among friends who will not denounce us to the authorities."

"Oh, they won't dare to arrest us," the fair Rebecca petulantly reassured her father.

At this point, the tall, grave, old Isaac d'Acosta raised his hand with a courtly southern gesture, and secured the attention of the gathering.

"If I may be permitted to voice my sentiments," he intervened, "I cheerfully lend approval to the proposal of our host. Yes, that little lady is quite right. Hanukkah means dedication. It is the Feast of Dedication. The Maccabean heroes rededicated the altar of God at Jerusalem on Hanukkah. And thus we too, American Jews engaged in a heroic struggle together with our fellow Americans, in the defense of our freedom — what better occasion to dedicate our sanctuary — our first synagogue than on Hanukkah?"

The company at the table looked at one another and nodded in approbation.

"Well spoken, brother," Bernard Gratz commented aloud. "Indeed there can be no more auspicious occasion."

And Haym Salomon, a gleam of pride in his dreamy eyes, rose from his seat.

"Hanukkah it must be," he burst out, "We shall dedicate our Shuhl to the triumph of our cause. Aye, Hanukkah it must be."

"Franks and Levy exchanged quizzical smiles, but said nothing.

"Then we must begin preparations right now," the beaming Josephson stated. "We must get also a Hanukkah Menorah, and wax candles — and — has anyone among us a Menorah — a big, silver Hanukkah Menorah brought over from the Old Country, maybe?"

It developed that there wasn't any Menorah to be produced.

"Well, I presume a Menorah was a bit too much of a luxury to fetch along in my little bundle when I came over on the good ship Queen Elizabeth."

Michael Gratz grinned, good-humouredly.

"We have a Menorah, a massive, silver Menorah over at Charleston," d'Acosta mused aloud. "I myself brought it across from Lisbon. But the congregation will want to make use of it on the festival. In any event, the line of communication has been broken. The British troops patrol the coastline. We cannot send for a Menorah all that distance."

It was finally Rebecca Gratz who offered the solution:

"I know where we can get a really beautiful Hanukkah Menorah," the young girl spoke up happily. "I saw one last winter in New York at the Shearith Israel Synagogue on Mills Street. The rabbi lit it on Hanukkah night."

"The New York Shuhl is closed," Mr. Salomon reminded them. "The Menorah isn't there any longer. I saw Rabbi Seixas take it away with him when he fled into the Connecticut Colony."

"Ho, Ho," Josephson suddenly exclaimed and struck the table in glee.

"I have got a magnificent proposition. We'll fetch Rabbi Seixas over here from Connecticut and we'll have him bring the Menorah with him."

"We're going to dedicate a Shuhl," he continued, "aren't we? And a Shuhl needs a rabbi. Rabbi Seixas can't go back to New York, not so long as the Britishers hold the city. There is nothing to hold him there in the Yankee village." He turned about to face a young guest, dressed in a Whig officer's uniform.

"Lieutenant Franks, you're going back to Valley Forge tomorrow, aren't you?"

"Yes, Mr. Josephson," Lieutenant Isaac Franks, aide de camp to General Washington, answered. "If I can be of any service?"

"Then it is all settled," Josephson announced with an air of finality. "You, lieutenant, can obtain from the General a convoy, proceed to Stratford in Connecticut, fetch Rabbi Seixas over here to us — with his Menorah and everything — and next Thursday night we shall celebrate Hanukkah and at the same time dedicate the site of our synagogue."

———————

And in this wise the first Hanukkah was celebrated in Old Philadelphia in those hectic days of the American Revolution. And it marked the dedication of Philadelphia's first synagogue by the Congregation Mikveh Israel, by Manuel Josephson, its first Parness or President, and by Rabbi Gershon Mendes Seixas, the refugee New York Rabbi — as its first rabbi.

The Little Hanukkah Lamp

I. L. Peretz

Well, well, so it's Hanukkah today. Maybe I'll tell you the story of a Jew, Shlome-Zalman by name, who was once rich, lost everything, (may such a thing never happen to you) and was saved from lifelong poverty by — guess what? By a Hanukkah lamp!

You are probably thinking that this little Hanukkah lamp was made of gold. Nonsense! It wasn't even a silver lamp. Just a plain broken-down brass lamp that had been in the family for generations. It was bent and crooked and one of the branches was split halfway down the center.

Mr. Shlome-Zalman had been an ordinary businessman. Suddenly he became very rich. How did he become rich? Don't ask me, because it has nothing to do with the story. But one thing I can tell you. As soon as he made a lot of money he began to turn the world upside down. He and his wife changed the style of their clothes. He bought only Berlin styles and his wife followed the Parisian fashions of the day. He took his boys out of Hebrew School and sent them to the Polish High School.

Of course they turned their house inside out. They had an old bookcase full of sacred Hebrew books. Who needed them now? They gave them to the synagogue library as a present. The bookcase they chopped into kindling for the fire and in its place they hung a full length mirror. They then called in a junkman sold him the old furniture for next to nothing and bought instead Louis XIV antiques. The chairs were so fine and dainty that people were afraid to sit down on them.

They even got rid of some of their silver ceremonial objects — spice boxes and citron holders — sold them for a pittance or gave them away as wedding presents to poor relatives. Then they bought fine china, crystal decanters and modern vases.

But the earth is a revolving planet; its fortunes go round and round. Before long Shlome-Zalman's luck took a bad turn. Soon he couldn't afford to send any more money to his two sons who were abroad. He couldn't pay his bills and no one would lend him any money. His situation went from bad to worse. He looked around the house for something to pawn. But the Louis XIV furniture had fallen apart and the china and crystal were chipped. Everything of value was gone!

They lived in great poverty. The worse it became the more they began to remember their Jewishness. Shlome-Zalman's wife borrowed a prayer-book from a neighbor. Shlome-Zalman himself, who was Mr. Solomon when he was rich and now used his old name, went to the synagogue and began to recite his prayers regularly.

When Hanukkah came around he had a strong desire to kindle the Hanukkah lights and pronounce the blessing. Somewhere they found Hanukkah candles. Then they went into the kitchen to look for something to put them on. But there was nothing — not even a bare piece of wood.

Suddenly Shlome-Zalman remembered their crooked old Hanukkah lamp which he had thrown on top of the oven.

"Shlome-Zalman," he wife pleaded, "climb up and find it."

So, risking life and limb, he climbed up on the table, then on to a wobbly Louis XIV chair, and brought the Hanukkah lamp down safely.

It was covered with layers of dust and needed plenty of cleaning. Finally it was polished. Shlome-Zalman lit the candles and recited the Hanukkah blessings.

And so it was for eight nights!

At the end of that time they were sitting and wondering where their next meal was coming from, when they heard a loud knock at the door. In came a young man, an acquaintance of theirs who was an antique dealer — he bought and sold all kinds of things.

"What are you doing here?" they asked him.

The dealer couldn't stop laughing.

"There's a crazy Englishman visiting in Warsaw. He is buying up all kinds of old rubbish — as a matter of fact he's waiting in the hall right now."

"Let him come in," said Shlome-Zalman.

"There must be something here we can sell him." They looked around — what old things did they have left to sell to the mad Englishman?

In the meantime the Englishman came in, took off his fur hat, looked around the room and caught sight of the Hanukkah lamp. He took hold of it with trembling hands and his eyes shone.

"I told you he's crazy," whispered the dealer.

"How much do you want for this?" asked the Englishman in broken German.

To make a long story short they sold him their Hanukkah lamp at a good price. When the Englishman and the dealer had gone, Shlome-Zalman exclaimed.

"He must be crazy — there's no other explanation."

"Maybe it was Elijah, the Prophet" said his wife.

Whatever it was, the money the Englishman paid them brought them luck. Once more Shlome-Zalman became rich and began calling himself Mr. Solomon. Good luck brings more good luck. Their children out in the world were doing well. The son in London had become an architect and had gotten married. He invited the father and mother to come to London to meet their daughter-in-law.

In London they saw everything — public buildings, shops, theatres, concert halls and exhibitions. One day they were taken to an art museum and — what's this? Under a glass case with a label underneath it, they came face to face with their own Hanukkah lamp, bent and crooked, with one of the branches split halfway down the center.

"So the Englishman wasn't crazy after all," said Mr. Solomon.

"And he wasn't Elijah the prophet," added Mrs. Solomon.

To talk about this lamp, or to ask questions about it in front of their young daughter-in-law, that would hardly be in good taste.

So each began to think about it silently.

And perhaps you are thinking too. . .

Reuben Lights a Torch

Sol Klein

He stood so still that at first he seemed only a deeper part of the darkness.

"Reuben?" she whispered softly.

He turned, and they made their way to each other across the flat roof of the house. A cloud moved over the moon, and a chill wind crept down from the hills of Judea.

"Reuben," she said, "you haven't been thinking of it again?"

"Yes, mother."

"Reuben, I can't let you go. They'll kill you, as they killed your father."

"They won't catch me," he said. "They are heavy men, and I am light of foot."

"They are many and we are few," she said without hearing him.

Gently, he took her hand and stood beside her.

"Look, mother," he said, "what do you see?"

"Only darkness."

"Only darkness," he repeated, "in our bright city of Jerusalem. Before they came, lights danced on our streets and highways."

"You are only a child," she said dully.

"Mother," he said, "listen. What do you hear?"

"Only the wind, my son."

"Listen," he said again.

"From the houses where the enemy dwells," she said, "I hear the sound of laughter."

"From the Syrians," he picked up her words, "the sound of drunken laughter. Who but the enemy laughs in the city of Jerusalem, while we cringe like mice on our dark roofs at night. I must go, mother. I am only a child in your eyes, but my place is with Judah."

The cloud slipped from the face of the moon. Under the yellow light Jerusalem lay silent, like a dead city.

"Go," she said at last, "you are a man. Your place is with Judah."

For a moment they clung to each other, then he seemed to melt from her side. She heard the sound of his feet as he made his way from the roof of the house. She saw him glide like a shadow through the slumbering streets. Then he was gone, and she felt a quiet joy as she had never known before. He was only a boy, but she had given a soldier to Judah Maccabee.

Reuben picked his way through the twisting streets, for he knew the city well. He knew where there were heavy trees to give him shelter, and he knew the narrow alleys where he could melt into the shadows. He knew where the Syrians slept, and where they came at night to drink and shout.

At last he reached the outskirts of the city. He sprinted across an open field and beyond it to the highway.

On and on he ran through the night, the wind singing through his hair. Dawn was rising when he cleared a bend in the road. With a startled cry he froze in his tracks. He was face to face with a company of enemy troops. Before he could move, rough hands reached out and seized him. Questions were rained upon him from every side.

"Why did you cry out, young one?"

"Surprised were you, like a deer coming upon a hunter?"

"Or it might be, like a spy for your Judah, son of Mattathias."

"Speak! What are you doing at this hour along an empty road?"

"Silence!" a stern voice suddenly broke into the babble of voices.

Reuben found himself looking up at the captain of the company, a heavy-faced man with grey eyes embedded in puffs of flesh.

"We are no fools," the captain told the boy. "We know you Judeans are ready to die rather than utter a word. You are on your way to Judah Maccabee. Speak, am I wrong?"

"You are not wrong," Reuben said quietly. "I would die rather than utter a word to comfort my people's tormentors."

"A brave lad," the captain said with a short laugh. "But you shall not die. We have need of lads like you to see that our helmets shine and our tents are in order. There are many ways of serving Antiochus."

Once more rude hands seized the boy, and the company marched on down the road. After an hour they turned into a lane that led to a forest. Among the trees stood rows of enemy tents. Men were moving about, rubbing the sleep from their eyes and preparing their morning meal.

The captain called Reuben into his tent. The restless grey eyes looked the boy up and down.

"You seem a healthy lad," he said at last. "That is well, for there is much work to be done. While the men eat, you shall clean their tents. If you shirk your tasks, we have ways of punishing which will make even a brave son of Judea cry out."

Reuben turned to go, when again the Syrian spoke.

"It will please you to hear," he said slowly, "that your Maccabees plan a raid upon us this night. Our spies have not been idle. When your friends attack, we shall be prepared to receive them." And with a wave of the hand, he dismissed the boy and sprawled out to rest on a mat in a corner of the tent.

Silently Reuben made his way among the men, who followed him with hard, curious eyes and taunting shouts. But Reuben felt nothing but the boring eyes of the captain. And in his ears his words echoed like drum beats: "We shall be prepared to receive them."

Reuben moved from tent to tent, straightening mats and piles of clothes. As he worked his mind raced feverishly. How to warn them! They would descend upon a camp which they thought asleep, and armed men would leap from trees, their weapons raised to strike. On the silent roof-top, his mother had said he was a man. But he was only a boy who had walked into the hands of the enemy.

When the tents were tidy Reuben was given piles of helmets to shine. Soldiers came and went, preparing for the night raid. One of them brushed against the boy as he sat before a tent and stumbled, dropping an unlit torch he was carrying.

"Out of the way!" he said angrily, and recovering his balance, he walked on, muttering under his breath. Reuben stared at the torch, his heart beating out a sudden hope. Quickly he glanced about him. No one was looking his way. He crawled forward slowly, picked up the torch, and tucked it into the loose folds of his tunic. The next instant he was back among the helmets.

The day wore slowly on. When evening came, the captain called his men together and gave them their last instructions. In the shadows Reuben stood, trying to still the beating of his heart. He had hidden the torch in the small tent where he was to sleep alone. If they discovered it they would kill him. But he had told his mother he was a soldier. A curt command from the captain, and the men dispersed to take their positions.

Reuben went to his tent and lay waiting in the dark. The moments crept by, and the hours. Utter silence around him. Sleep tugged at his eyes. With the palms of his hands he beat his temples to keep himself awake.

Then it came. Footfalls like distant whispers. The Syrians stirred in the trees, setting the leaves whimpering. Nearer they came, the feet of the Maccabees, muffled thuds creeping down from the hills.

Reuben strained his ears till the blood throbbed in his head. Nearer came the stealthy march of feet. The march of freedom from the hilltops, from the deep caverns, from the secret places of the land.

The camp stirred softly, like a beast awaking from sleep. Reuben crept to the door of his tent. Vague shadows loomed beyond the camp. The shadows grew larger, drew closer and closer.

Reuben grasped his torch.

"Mother!" his lips quivered. "Mother!"

And then his hands grew firm. Another instant, and the torch flared, a jet of flame in the dark.

"Brothers!" he shouted. "The enemy is prepared."

Shouts of fear and anger rang through the trees. Men leaped to seize him, but the boy darted like a hare between their hands. A spear whirred past his ear, and Reuben threw the torch to the ground and stamped out its flame. Again the darkness shielded him as he fled to the edge of the encampment, into the arms of the Maccabees.

The battle raged till dawn. When the sun rose, a weary band of Maccabees made its way triumphantly back to the hills. At their head walked Judah Maccabee, and beside him was the young lad from Jerusalem, his face turned to the sun.

Reb Yudel's Hanukkah

David Einhorn

Hanukkah candles sometimes do unexpected things. We know of one man whose life was saved by the little candles that are lit on this festival of freedom.

It happened many years ago, and the hero of the story was Reb Yudel. The whole town knew Reb Yudel. He was a wealthy lumber merchant, and beloved by the community. Of course he was a pious Jew, and he gave a great deal of charity to the deserving poor. But the one Jewish custom which he loved above all others was that of lighting the orange Hanukkah candles which commemorated the rededication of the Temple.

Now Reb Yudel's affairs were such that he spent most of his time on the road, traveling from one customer to another. And whenever Hanukkah approached, he always made certain to keep with him a supply of little candles, so that he might never be caught unprepared when the time came to say "Al Hanisim."

This year Reb Yudel was especially happy because it was already the sixth day of Hanukkah and he had thus far been able to remain at home, spinning the dreidel with his children, eating the wonderful latkes his wife Malkah prepared for him.

But suddenly a special messenger arrived with disheartening news. Business called and Reb Yudel had to be off again, this time to visit a Polish noble whose castle was several days travel away. Reb Yudel packed his clothes, filled two money bags with gold pieces, took along his little candles and climbed into the carriage. His driver was a Polish peasant who had always lived in that neighborhood, an old native who could almost make his way blindfolded through the forest. When he saw Reb Yudel carry his money bags into the carriage, he craftily decided to lead his passenger astray in the woods. He planned to leave him there alone all night, in the hope that he would be devoured by wild animals. When that happened, the driver decided, he would be able to make off with Reb Yudel's bags of gold.

They drove and drove until night fell. When the driver saw that it was pitch dark, he descended from his seat and fled into the blackness, leaving his employer alone and completely lost. Reb Yudel felt his way about and managed to stumble into a little clearing hidden in a clump of trees. Leaving himself to the mercy of God, he prepared to spend the night there.

Suddenly he remembered that it was Hanukkah and he took the little box of candles out of his bag. He cleared off the snow from the branch of a spruce tree and firmly fastening seven candles on the branch, he said his evening prayers and lit the Hanukkah candles.

He had barely finished praying when a strange feeling swept over him. Looking up, he saw himself surrounded by the gleaming eyes of hungry wolves. They had formed a circle outside his little clearing and were slowly inching their way towards him. Just then the little candles flared up with a mighty flame. The snowflakes on the spruce tree reflected the fire as though the clearing were full of a hundred mirrors. The wolves stopped in their tracks, frightened by the blinding glare. And so the seven little wax candles burnt brightly through the long winter night, and the wolves kept their distance.

When dawn broke, the wolves slunk away to their lairs. Reb Yudel climbed up into the carriage and drove through the forest until he finally reached the noble's castle. Several days later the wicked driver was found lying under a tall pine tree. While waiting for Reb Yudel to be eaten by the wild beasts, he had frozen to death.

Glossary for Hanukkah Money

Al-kein n'Kave lecho: The beginning of the second part of the prayer Oleinu "Therefore we hope. . . . "

Bar Mitzvah: A thirteen year-old Jewish boy who is confirmed; the confirmation ceremony itself.

cheder: Old-style orthodox Hebrew school.

dreidel: a small top, spun with the fingers, and played with by children on Hanukkah.

Gamorah: The Aramaic name for the Talmud, a compilation of the religious, ethical and legal teachings and decisions interpreting the Bible.

grivnye: Silver coin worth ten Kopeks.

groschen: Small German silver coin whose old value was about two cents.

gulden: An Austrian silver florin worth about forty-eight cents.

kopek: A small copper coin; there are 100 kopeks in a ruble.

Oleinu: Literally, "it is our duty", the last prayer in the daily Jewish liturgy.

piatekas: Five-Kopek pieces.

ruble: Formerly a Russian silver coin, later a piece of paper money.

Shehu noteh shomayim: Literally, "who stretched forth the heavens", from the Oleinu prayer.

shammes: Sexton.

shi-shi: Sixth part of the scriptural portion for the week read aloud on the Sabbath in the synagogue, and regarded as a great honor for the reader.

shkotzim: Good-for-nothings.

tallis: Prayer-shawl.

tfillin: Phylacteries.

Hanukkah Money

Sholom Aleichem

Can you guess, children, which is the best of all holidays? *Hanukkah*, of course.

You don't go to *cheder* for eight days in a row, you eat pancakes every day, spin your *dreidel* to your heart's content and from all sides *Hanukkah* money comes pouring in. What holiday could be better than that?

Winter. Outside it's cold, a bitter frost. The windows are frozen over, decorated with beautiful designs, the sills piled high with snow. Inside the house it's warm and cheerful. The silver *Hanukkah* lamp stands ready on the table and my father is walking back and forth, his hands behind his back, saying the evening prayers. When he is almost through, but while still praying, he takes out of the chest a waxen candle (the *shammes*, to light the others with) and starting *Oleinu*, the last prayer in the regular services, signals to us:

" '*Shehu noteh shomayim . . .*' *Nu! Nu-o!*"

My brother and I don't know what he means. We ask, "What do you want? A match?"

My father points with his hand toward the kitchen door, " '*Alkein n'kaveh l'cho . . .*' *E-o-nu!*"

"What then? A bread knife? Scissors? The mortar and pestle?"

My father shakes his head. He makes a face at us, comes to the end of the prayer, and then, able to speak again, says, "Your mother! Call your mother! I'm ready to light the candles!"

The two of us, my brother and I, leap for the kitchen, almost falling over each other in our haste.

"Mother! Quick! The *Hanukkah* candles!"

"Oh, my goodness! Here I am! *Hanukkah* lights!" cries my mother, leaving her work in the kitchen (rendering goose fat, mixing batter for pancakes), and hurries into the parlor with us. And after her comes Braina the cook, a swarthy woman with a round plump face and mustache, her hands always smeared with grease. My mother stands at one side of the room with a pious look on her face, and Braina the cook remains at the door, wipes her hand on her

dirty apron, draws her greasy hand over her nose, and leaves a black smear across her face.

My father goes up to the lamp with his lighted candle, bends down and sings in the familiar tune, "Blessed art thou, O Lord . . ." and ends " . . . to kindle the lights of *Hanukkah*."

My mother, in her most pious voice, chimes in, "Blessed be He and blessed be His name." And later, "Amen." Braina nods her approval and makes such queer faces that Motel and I are afraid to look at each other.

"These lights we kindle," my father continues, marching up and down the room with an eye on the *Hanukkah* lamp. He keeps up this chant till we grow impatient and wish that he would reach his hand into his pocket and take out his purse. We wink at each other, nudge and push each other.

"Motel," I say, "go ask him for *Hanukkah* money."

"Why should I ask?"

"Because you're younger. That's why."

"That's why I shouldn't. You go. You're older."

My father is well aware of what we are talking about, but he pretends not to hear. Quietly, without haste, he walks over to the cupboard and begins to count out some money. A cold shiver runs down our backs, our hands shake, our hearts pound. We look up at the ceiling, scratch our earlocks, try to act as if this meant nothing at all to us.

My father coughs.

"H'm . . . Children, come here."

"Huh? What is it?"

"Here is *Hanukkah* money for you."

The money in our pockets, we move off, Motel and I, at first slowly, stiffly, like toy soldiers, then faster and faster with a skip and a hop. And before we have reached our room we lose all restraint and turn three somersaults one after the other. Then hopping on one foot we sing:

> *"Einga beinga*
> *Stupa tzeinga*
> *Artze bartze*
> *Gola shwartze*
> *Eimelu reimelu*
> *Beigeli feigeli*
> *Hop!"*

And in our great joy and exuberance we slap our own cheeks twice, so hard that they tingle.

The door opens and in walks Uncle Benny.

"Come here, you rascals. I owe you some *Hanukkah* money."

Uncle Benny puts his hand into his vest pocket, takes out two silver *gulden*, and gives us each one.

Nobody in the world would ever guess that our father and Uncle Benny are brothers. My father is tall and thin; my uncle is short and fat. My father is dark, my uncle is fair. My father is gloomy and silent, my uncle jolly and talkative. As different as day and night, summer and winter. And yet they are blood brothers.

My father takes a large sheet of paper ruled off into squares, black and white, and asks us to bring him a handful of dry beans from the kitchen, dark ones and white ones. They are going to play checkers.

(Once a miracle happened, and this is our celebration.)

Mother is in the kitchen rendering goose fat and frying pancakes. My brother and I are spinning our *dreidel*. My father and Uncle Benny sit down and play checkers.

"One thing I'll have to ask you," my father says. "Once you've made a move it's a move. You can't keep changing your mind."

"A move is a move," my uncle agrees, and makes a move.

"A move is a move," repeats my father and jumps my uncle's bean.

"That's right," says Uncle Benny, "a move is a move," and jumps twice.

The longer they play the more absorbed they become. They chew their beards, beat time under the table with their feet, and together they hum one song.

"Oh, what shall I do? What shall I do? What shall I do?" sings my father, chewing an end of his beard. "If I move here," he chants, as one does over the *Gemara*, "then he'll move there. Maybe I'd better move . . . over here."

"Over here . . . over here," echoes Uncle Benny in the same tone.

"Why should I worry?" my father hums again. "If he should take this *one* then I'll take those *two*. On the other hand, maybe he thinks he can take three . . ."

"Take three . . . take three . . . take three . . ." Uncle Benny helps him out.

"Ah, you're no good, Benny. You're no good at all," sings my father and makes a move.

"You're worse than no good, my brother," sings Uncle Benny and pushes a bean forward, then snatches it back.

"You can't do that, Benny," my father cries. "You said a move was a move!" And he catches Uncle Benny's hand.

"No!" Uncle Benny insists. "If I haven't finished I can still move."

"No!" my father declares just as emphatically. "We decided on that before we started. Remember. You can't change your mind."

"I can't?" asks Uncle Benny. "How many times did you change yours?"

"I?" says my father indignantly. "See! That's why I hate to play with you, Benny!"

"Who is forcing you to play with me?"

At this point my mother comes in from the kitchen, her face flaming from the heat.

"Already? Fighting already?" she asks. "Over a few beans?"

Behind her comes Braina with a large platter of steaming pancakes. We all move toward the table. My brother Motel and I, who only a moment ago had been fighting like cat and dog, make up quickly, become friends again, and go after the pancakes with the greatest gusto.

In bed that night I lie awake and think: how much would I be worth if all my uncles and aunts and other relatives gave me *Hanukkah* money? First of all there is Uncle Moishe-Aaron, my mother's brother, stingy but rich. Then Uncle Itzy and Aunt Dveira, with whom my father and mother have not been on speaking terms for years and years. Then Uncle Beinish and Aunt Yenta. And how about our sister Ida and her husband Sholom-Zeidel? And all the other relatives?

"Motel, are you asleep?"

Yes. What do you want?"

"How much *Hanukkah* money do you think Uncle Moishe-Aaron will give us?"

"How should I know? I'm not a prophet."

A minute later: "Motel, are you sleeping?"

"Yes. What now?"

"Do you think anyone else in the whole world has as many uncles and aunts as we have?"

"Maybe yes . . . and maybe no."

Two minutes later: "Motel, are you asleep?"

"Of course."

"If you're asleep, how can you talk to me?"

"You keep bothering me so I have to answer."

Three minutes later: "Motel, are you awake?"

This time he answers with a snore. I sit up in bed, take out my father's present, smooth it out, examine it. A whole *ruble*.

"Think of it," I said to myself. "A piece of paper, and what can't you buy with it! Toys, knives, canes, purses, nuts and candy, raisins, figs. Everything."

I hide the *ruble* under my pillow and say my prayers. A little later Braina comes in from the kitchen with a platter full of *rubles* . . . She isn't walking, she's floating in the air, chanting, "These lights we kindle . . ." And Motel begins to swallow *rubles* as if they were pancakes.

"Motel!" I scream with all my might. "God help you, Motel! What are you doing? Eating money?"

I sit up with a start . . . spit three times. It was a dream.

And I fall asleep again.

The next morning after we have said our prayers and eaten breakfast, our mother puts on our fur-lined jackets and bundles us up in warm shawls and we start off for our *Hanukkah* money. First of all, naturally, we stop off at Uncle Moishe-Aaron's.

Our Uncle Moishe-Aaron is a sickly man. He has trouble with his bowels. Whenever we come we find him at the wash bowl after having come in from the back yard, washing and drying his hands with the appropriate prayer.

"Good morning, Uncle Moishe-Aaron!" we cry out together, my brother and I. Our Aunt Pessil, a tiny woman with one black eyebrow and one white one, comes forward to meet us. She takes off our coats, unwinds our shawls, and proceeds to blow our noses into her apron.

"Blow!" says Aunt Pessil. "Blow hard. Don't be afraid. Again! Again! That's the way!"

And Uncle Moishe-Aaron, a little man with a motheaten mustache and ears stuffed with cotton, dressed in his old ragged fur-lined jacket and with his quilted skullcap on his head, stands at the wash bowl, wiping his hands, wrinkling his face, blinking at us with his eyes, while he groans out his prayer.

My brother and I sit down uneasily. We are always miserable and frightened in this house. Aunt Pessil sits opposite us, her arms folded across her chest, and put us through her usual examination.

"How is your father?"

"All right."

"And your mother?"

"All right."

"Have they killed any geese yet?"

"Oh, yes."

"Did they have much fat?"

"Quite a lot."

" Did your mother make pancakes yet?"

"Yes."

"Has Uncle Benny come yet?"

"Yes."

"Did they play checkers?"

"Yes."

And so on and so on . . .

Aunt Pessil blows our noses again and turns to Uncle Moishe-Aaron.

"Moishe-Aaron, we ought to give the children some *Hanukkah* money."

Uncle Moishe-Aaron doesn't hear. He keeps on drying his hands, and comes to the end of his prayer with a drawn-out groan.

Aunt Pessil repeats: "Moishe-Aaron! The children! *Hanukkah* money."

"Huh? What?" says Uncle Moishe-Aaron, and shifts the cotton from one ear to the other.

"The children. *Hanukkah* money!" Aunt Pessil shouts right into his ear.

"Oh, my bowels, my bowels," groans Uncle Moishe-Aaron (that's the way he always talks), holding his belly with both hands. "Did you say *Hanukkah* money? What do children need money for? What will you do with it, huh? Spend it? Squander it? How much did your father give you? Huh?"

"He gave me a *ruble*," I say, "and him a half."

"A *ruble!* Hm . . . Some people spoil their children, ruin them. What will you with the *ruble*, huh!? Change it? Huh? No! Don't change it. Do you hear what I say? Don't change it. Or do you want to change it? Huh?"

"What does it matter to you whether they change it or don't change it?" breaks in Aunt Pessil. "Give them what they have coming and let them go on their way."

Uncle Moishe-Aaron shuffles off to his room and begins to search through all the chests and drawers, finds a coin here, a coin there, and mutters to himself:

"Hm . . . How they spoil their children. Ruin them. Simply ruin them."

And coming back, he pushes a few hard coins into our hands. Once more (for the last time) Aunt Pessil blows our noses, puts on our coats, wraps the shawls around us, and we go on our way. We run over the white frozen crunchy snow, counting the money that Uncle Moishe-Aaron has given us. Our hands are frozen, red and stiff. The coins are copper, large and heavy, very old six-*kopek* pieces, strange, old-fashioned three-*kopek* pieces rubbed smooth and thin, *groschens* that we've never seen before, thick and green with age. It's hard for us, in fact impossible, to figure out how much *Hannukah* money Uncle Moishe-Aaron has given us.

Our second stop for *Hanukkah* money is at Uncle Itzy's and Aunt Dveira's, with whom my parents have not been on speaking terms for many years. Why they don't speak to each other I don't know, but I do know that they never speak, although they go to the same synagogue and sit next to each other on the same bench. And at the holidays when it comes to auctioning off the various honors, they always try to outbid each other. A fierce battle takes place each time. The whole congregation takes sides, helps them to bid, eggs them on.

The *shammes*, who acts as auctioneer, stands on the platform, working hard. His skullcap is off to one side, his prayer-shawl keeps slipping off his shoulders.

"Eighteen *gulden* for *Shi-shi!*"

"Twenty *gulden* for *Shi-shi!*"

The bidding gets hotter and hotter. My father and Uncle Itzy are bent over their Bibles, from all appearances unaware of what is going on. But every time one of them bids the other one raises it.

The congregation enjoys the spectacle and helps along. "Thirty . . . thirty-five . . . thirty-seven and a half . . ." But the battle is between my father and Uncle Itzy, and they continue the bidding until one or the other has to give up.

And yet whenever there is a celebration in the family, a birth, a circumcision, a *Bar Mitzvah*, an engagement party, a wedding or a divorce, the feud is forgotten. We all attend, exchange gifts, make merry, drink together and dance together like the best of friends.

"Good morning, Uncle Itzy! Good morning. Aunt Dveira!" we cry out together, my brother Motel and I, and they receive us like honored guests.

"Did you come all this way just to see us, or was there something else on your mind?" Uncle Itzy asks and pinches our cheeks. He opens his purse and gives us our *Hanukkah* money, a new silver twenty-*kopek* piece to me and another one to my brother. And from there we go straight to Uncle Beinish's.

If you want a picture of complete chaos, go to our Uncle Beinish's house. No matter when you come you find a perfect bedlam. They have a house full of children, half-naked, dirty, unkempt, unwashed, always bruised, usually scratched, often bloodied and with black eyes. One of the children may be laughing, another crying; one singing, another shrieking; one humming, another whistling; this one has put on his father's coat with the sleeves rolled up, and that one is riding a broomstick; this one is drinking milk from a pitcher, that one is cracking nuts, another is walking about with a herring's head in his hand, and still another is sucking on a stick of candy while from his nose two runnels flow down toward his mouth. Aunt Yenta must be strong as an ox to put up with this crew. She curses them, pinches them, shakes them all day long. She isn't particular. Whichever one comes within reach gets a slap or a shove or a prod in the side.

An ordinary slap by itself is not worth mentioning. "I hope you choke; I hope you die; why doesn't someone kidnap you!" These are the lesser curses. And words like "the plague" and "cholera" and "violent death" are uttered casually, without anger, as one might say "Good evening" or "Good Sabbath." The house becomes quiet only when Uncle Beinish comes home. But since Uncle Beinish is a busy man who spends all his time at the store, coming home only for meals, their house is a perpetual Gehenna.

When we come in we find little Ezriel riding on his older brother

Getzi's back with Froike and Mendel whipping Getzi on, one with the sleeve of an old jacket, the other with the cover of a prayer book. Chaim'l, who has found the windpipe of a slaughtered goose somewhere, is blowing at it until he is blue in the face, and succeeds in producing an eerie sound like the squeal of a stuck pig. Zeinvilleh is playing a tune on a comb and David, a small boy of about four, has put his shoes on his hands and beats time with them. Sender'l rushes by carrying a kitten by the scruff of the neck. The kitten's tongue hangs out, its eyes are shut, its feet hang limply. You can almost hear it say, "See how I suffer here; they torture me, they make life unbearable." In another corner Esther, the oldest girl, is trying to comb and braid her little sister Haska's hair, but since the hair is curly and has not been combed for a long time, the child stands shrieking at the top of her voice and Esther keeps slapping her to make her stop. The only quiet one is Pinny, a tiny boy with crooked legs, his shirt tail pinned up behind him. The only trouble with him is that wherever he goes he leaves a trail behind him.

But none of this disturbs Aunt Yenta in the least. It does not prevent her from sitting calmly at the table drinking chicory, with an infant at her breast and an older child on her knee. Between sips of chicory she cuddles the baby at her breast and digs her elbow into the child on her knee. "Look at you eat, you pig! May the worms eat you! Esther, Rochel, Haska, where the devil are you? Quick, wipe his nose! Bring me a saucer, quick! Here I am, drinking without a saucer! Mendel, don't make so much noise! I'll give you such a crack that you'll turn over three times! Oh, my heart, my soul, my comfort. What, murderers, you want more food? All you do all day is eat, eat, eat! Why don't you choke!"

When they catch sight of the two of us the children fall on us like locusts, grabbing us by our hands, our feet, some leaping at our heads. Chaim'l blows the windpipe right into my ear. David, still wearing his shoes on his hands, throws his arms around us. Pinny, with the shirt tail pinned behind him, gets hold of one of my legs and wraps himself about it like a little snake. A confusion of sounds and voices surrounds us, deafens our ears.

"May you scream with a toothache!" shouts Aunt Yenta from the other room. "A person can get deaf here! They're devils, not children! May your souls burn forever and ever!"

And in the midst of all this noise and confusion Uncle Beinish comes in with his *tallis* and *tfillin*, apparently on his way from the synagogue, and at once everything becomes quiet. The children vanish.

"Good morning, Uncle Beinish!" we cry out together, my brother

Motel and I.

"What are you doing, here you *shkotzim*" asks Uncle Beinish. "Ah, *Hanukkah* money!" And he gives us each a ten-*kopek* piece.

The children peek at us from their corners with bright little eyes like mice, wink and signal with their hands, make strange faces at us, try hard to make us laugh. But with great effort we control ourselves, take the money, and run off as fast as we can from this living Gehenna.

The next place we go to for *Hanukkah* money is our sister Ida's. Since she was a child Ida has always been a lugubrious creature. No matter what silly little thing happened, she could always be counted on to burst out crying. She was always shedding tears over her own or other people's troubles. But when she became engaged to Sholom-Zeidel, that was when she really cried! Perhaps you think it was because the young man didn't please her? God forbid! She had never even seen the man! No, she wept because a bride is supposed to weep before her wedding. When the tailors brought her trousseau she wept all night long. Later, when her girl friends came for their last party together, she ran off to her room every few minutes to weep into her pillows. But she was really at her best on her wedding day! That day she didn't stop crying for a minute.

But the climax came at the veiling, when Menashe Fiddele, the fiddler, led her to the dais and Reb Boruch Badchen climbed up on the table, folded his arms over his ample stomach, lowered his head as though he were bemoaning the dead, and began, in a mournful tone that could move a stone to tears, the following song:

> *Dearest Bride, dearest bride!*
> *Weep all you please;*
> *Your tears are becoming,*
> *They need not cease.*
>
> *Weeping is ordained*
> *For brides to be.*
> *And soon you will stand*
> *Under the canopy.*
>
> *For you must learn*
> *That now your life*
> *Is full of sadness,*
> *Woe and strife;*

That man is not made
Of iron or stone,
He is only a being
Of flesh and bone,

That sinners are lashed
In the depths of hell,
And they scream and howl
And lament as well.

Then learn to practice virtue
And humility.
Weep, maiden, weep,
Let your tears run free.

And so on and so on without end.

The women who stood around her, helping to undo her beautiful long braids, could not control themselves. They gave themselves up to their lamentations wholeheartedly, made the oddest faces, wiped their eyes and blew their noses. And poor Ida wept loudest of all. She wailed and moaned and blubbered so hard that she fainted three times and they barely revived her in time for the ceremony.

But our brother-in-law, on the other hand, was as merry as our sister Ida was sad. If anything, Sholom-Zeidel was too merry, a practical joker, a clown, a zany, who fastened himself to you like a leech and got under your skin. He was always teasing us, my brother and me, pinching our ears and filliping our noses. That gave him his greatest pleasure. The first year they were married there were times when for days Motel and I went around with swollen noses, stinging ears. So when we heard that the young couple was leaving our home to set up their own establishment we were really overjoyed. But for the rest of the family the day they moved was a day of mourning. Ida wept, poured buckets of tears, and my mother, watching her, wept also. Sholom-Zeidel, who was supposed to be doing the packing, skipped back and forth, stole up behind us cunningly, and pinched our ears or filliped our noses. And when he bade us farewell he had the impudence to tell us not to wait to be invited but to come as often as we liked. We swore to each other on our honor, my brother and I, never to set foot in his house as long as we lived.

But a person forgets all things, even a pinched ear. How can you keep from going to your own married sister for *Hanukkah* money?

When we come into the house, Sholom-Zeidel greets us heartily.

"Well, well! Look who's here! I'm glad you came. I've been waiting: I have some *Hanukkah* money for you!"

76

And Sholom-Zeidel takes out his purse and hands each one of us several shiny silver coins. And before we can even count how many he has given us, his hand flies out, pinch, fillip go his fingers, and once more our ears and nose feel the sharp sting.

"Leave them alone! Haven't you tortured them enough?" our sister Ida begs him with tears in her eyes, and calling us aside, fills our pockets with cake, nuts and figs, and gives us *Hanukkah* money besides.

We make our escape as quickly as we can and hurry home.

"Well, Motel," I say, "let's get down to business. Let's figure out how much money we've collected. But I'll tell you what. You wait. First let me count mine and then you'll count yours."

And I begin to count. A ruble and three twenty-*kopek* pieces, four *gulden*, five *grivnye*, six *piatekas* . . . how much is that altogether? It must be a *ruble* and three twenties and four *gulden* and five *grivnye* and six *piatekas* . . .

My brother Motel won't wait until I am through, and he gets busy with his own finances. He moves each coin from one hand to the other and counts.

"A twenty and a twenty are two twenties, and one more is three. And two *gulden* is three twenties and two *gulden* and a *grivnye* and another *grivnye* and one more—that makes two twenties and three *gulden*, I mean three *gulden* and two twenties . . . What am I talking about? I'll have to start all over again from the beginning."

And he starts all over from the beginning. We count and we count and we can't get the total. We figure and we figure and we can't get it straight. When we get to Uncle Moishe-Aaron's old *piatekas*, huge sixes, smoothly rubbed threes, and swollen *groschens* we get so mixed up that we don't know where in the world we are. We try to exchange these coins with our mother, our father, with Braina the cook, but it doesn't work. Nobody wants to have anything to do with them.

"What sort of *piatekas* are those? Who palmed them off on you?"

We are ashamed to tell, and we keep quiet.

"Do you know what," says my brother Motel, "let's throw them into the oven, or outside in the snow, when no one is looking."

"What a smart boy you are!" I tell him. "It would be better to give them to a beggar."

But just to spite us no one comes to our door. We wait and we wait and not a single one appears. We can't get rid of Uncle Moishe-Aaron's present.

Food on Hanukkah

Jewish tradition specifically forbids fasting and mourning on Hanukkah. Since the very opposite of fasting and mourning are feasting and merry making, it is clear that food and fun go hand in hand with Hanukkah.

This is as it should be. Because when all is said and done, what would Hanukkah be without latkes?

The happy fact about this magnificent potato pancake is that it is not only simply delicious but deliciously simple to make. And so are many other tasty Hanukkah recipes.

The custom of eating latkes is so old that the reason for it is lost and forgotten. Some people have a theory which begins with cheese.

The theory is that when the custom originated, cheese pancakes were eaten on Hanukkah because, according to a legend, Judith, a daughter of the Hasmoneans, fed cheese to an enemy general. This made him thirsty for wine. Judith filled him with wine until he became drunk and fell asleep. Then she delivered him unto the hands of the Maccabees.

Whatever the reason, everyone will agree that it is better to eat latkes than to think about them. Otherwise they may get cold and soggy. And really, latkes are best when they are crisp and brown and sizzling hot, right out of the frying pan!

And now to all you latke fryers and latke eaters—

Good Cooking and Happy Eating!

Ingredients:

2 large potatoes
½ an onion
1 egg
¼ cup flour
1 teaspoon salt
oil, butter or shortening

Equipment:

grater
mixing bowl
beater
fry pan
spoon
paper toweling
spatula
measuring cup
paring knife

How to Make:

1. Peel the potatoes and grate.
2. Peel and grate the onion.
3. Add the flour, salt, and egg.
4. Mix thoroughly till smooth.
5. Grease the fry pan.
6. Drop the batter into the hot fry pan, making each pancake about three inches in diameter.
7. Fry till brown on one side; then turn to other side and also fry till brown.
8. Lift from fry pan and place on paper toweling till fat drains off.

Ingredients:

2 cups flour
1 cup sugar
½ teaspoon salt
2 teaspoons baking powder
1 egg
⅓ cup butter
¼ cup milk
1 teaspoon vanilla
butter, oil or shortening

Equipment:

large bowl
measuring cup
measuring spoon
beater
sifter
bread board
rolling pin
cookie cutters
cookie sheet

How to Make:

1. Cream butter and sugar in a large bowl.
2. In another bowl, beat the egg and add the milk and flavoring.
3. Stir both mixtures into a large bowl.
4. Sift together the flour, salt, and baking powder.
5. Add these ingredients to the large mixture and stir well.
6. Place the dough into the refrigerator for one hour.
7. Dust a bread board and rolling pin with flour.
8. Roll out the cool dough about ¼ of an inch thick.
9. Cut into fancy shapes with cookie cutters.
10. Place on greased cookie sheet.
11. Bake in oven for 12 minutes.

Ingredients:

¾ cup sugar
1 cup water
1 cup grapefruit juice
1 cup orange juice
1 cup pineapple juice
¼ cup lemon juice
1 quart ginger ale
Ice

Equipment:

Saucepan
Large mixing spoon
Strainer
Measuring cup
Punch bowl or any large bowl

Method:

Combine sugar and water in saucepan
Bring to boil
Stir until sugar dissolves
Turn heat down
Boil gently for 5 minutes
Cool

Before the Party:

Strain fruit juices
Combine strained juices
Add cooled sugar syrup
Add ginger ale
Just before serving pour into punch
    bowl containing ice
Decorate with orange and lemon slices
Serve 12 refreshing drinks

CHOCOLATE MARSHMALLOW SLICES

Ingredients:

24 marshmallows
4 oz. unsweetened chocolate
1 egg, beaten
1 cup confectioner's sugar
1 tsp. butter
1 cup chopped nuts
1 can shredded coconut

Equipment:

Mixing bowl
Double boiler
Knife
Measuring spoon
Measuring cup
Mixing spoon
3 pieces of waxed paper 12″ x 12″

Method:

Cut marshmallows into quarters
Melt chocolate and butter in double boiler
Combine marshmallows, sugar, beaten egg, nuts,
    melted chocolate and butter in bowl
Mix thoroughly until all ingredients are blended.
Be sure all the marshmallows are coated with chocolate.
Divide mixture into 3 portions
Roll each portion in coconut on waxed paper
Form into long coconut covered rolls
Wrap well and refrigerate until firm
Slice as needed with a sharp knife

Your hero's body is

A delicious double-decker sandwich
of

Chicken		Tomatoes
Turkey	a	Cucumbers
Salami		Pickles
Corned beef	n	Bermuda onion
Egg		Celery
Salmon	d	Lettuce
Cream cheese		Olives

with buttons of..Stuffed olives or radish slices, or nuts

His head is..A slice of tomato

His neck is..A stalk of celery

His arms and legs are..Carrot sticks

In his right hand he holds..An asparagus spear

Note: Any of the fillings in Column I can be deliciously combined with any of the vegetables in Column II.

MENORAH FRUIT SALAD

Place crisp lettuce leaf on plate

For base of menorah use..2 stalks of celery stuffed with cream cheese and nuts

For stem of menorah use..1 pear half

The menorah is..½ banana, sliced lengthwise

The candles are..pineapple spears

The flames are..Maraschino cherries

HANUKKAH PANCAKES

Ingredients:

one cup pancake mix
one cup milk
shortening, oil or butter
maple syrup

Equipment:

griddle
spatula
spoon
large bowl
paper toweling
measuring cup

How to Make:

1. To one cup of milk add one cup of pancake mix.
2. Stir well and leave no lumps.
3. Heat the griddle and grease with shortening, keep the heat on medium.
4. Spoon pancake mixture on to hot griddle; each pancake should be about four inches in diameter.
5. When edges look brown and the bubbles start to break, turn the pancake with your spatula.
6. Cook till brown on the other side.
7. Remove from skillet and serve with butter and syrup.

Songs and Prayers for Hanukkah

In a well-known operetta by Gilbert and Sullivan, a young prince disguises himself as a wandering minstrel and travels through his father's realm with a bag of "ballads, songs and snatches" in search of his lady love.

"My collection of songs is vast," he sings, "I can gear my tunes to any whim; I have a song for each occasion; I know a melody for every mood."

On Hanukkah we too, like the wandering minstrel, have a song for each occasion and a melody for every mood.

If you want a hymn of thanksgiving we have several!

If you need a melody for your Hanukkah blessing — it's here in this collection.

Do you want a song about a dreydel or a musical recipe for making latkes — we have those too.

So look through these pages. Then when spirits soar during your Hanukkah festivities and happy feelings need gay songs to express themselves, you will certainly have the songs you want, to sing the feelings you feel!

Hanukkah Blessings

Slowly

(solo) Bo — ruḥ a-to A — do — noy, Bo — ruḥ hu u — vo-
ruḥ sh' — mo, (solo) E — lo — he — nu me — leḥ ho-o — lom a — she-

sher ki-d'sho-nu b'-mitz-vo — sov v'-tzi-vo — nu l'
o — so ni-sim la-vo -sey — nu ba-yo — mim

had-lik ner shel Ha-nu — — koh. o — — men.
ho — — hem ba — — z'-man ha — ze.

(solo) she — he — he-yo — nu v'-ki — mo — nu v'-hi — gi-o-
nu laz' — man ha-ze. O — — — — — men.

Al Hanisim

90

ra - ḥa - - me- ḥo ho - ra - bim _____ o - ma - d'

2. D. C. al Fine

ro - som b' - rah - me - ḥo ho - ra - - bim. (Chorus)

Mooz Tzur

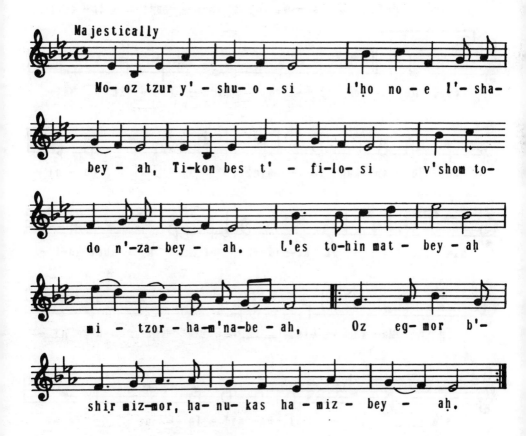

Majestically

Mo- oz tzur y' - shu - o - si l'ḥo no - e l' - sha -

bey - ah, Ti-kon bes t' - fi-lo- si v'shom to -

do n'-za- bey - ah. L'es to-hin mat - bey - ah

mi - tzor - ha-m'na-be - ah, Oz eg-mor b' -

shir miz-mor, ḥa- nu- kas ha - miz - bey - ah.

91

Y'mey Hanukkah

sher ho - l' - lu Ma - ka - bim. _____

Kemah Kemah

Ke-mah, ke-mah min ha-sak, she-men, she-men

min ha-kad. Ha-nu-kah ha-yom, Hag na-im neh-

mad! La la la la la la la la la la

la la la Ha-nu-kah ha-yom Hag na-im neh-

mad, La la la la la la la la la la la la

la la la la la la la la la la la la la

la la la la la la la la la la la.

Hanukkah Chag Yafeh Kol Kach

With spirit

Ha- nu - kah, ha- nu- kah, hag ya- fe kol kah.

Or ha - viv mi - sa- viv, gil l'- ye - led rah.

Ha - nu -kah, ha- nu-kah, s'- vi - von sov, sov,

sov, sov, sov, sov, sov,sov, Ma na - im va - tov.

Mi Y'malel

Very rhythmic

Mi y'-ma-lel g'vu – rot Yis-ra-el? O – tan mi yim – ne? Hen b'-hol dor ya – kum ha-gi-bor go – el ha – am. Sh'ma! Ba – ya-mim ha-hem baz'-man ha – ze, Ma-ka-bi mo-shi – a, u-fo – de. U-v'ya-mey-nu kol am Yis-ra – el Yit-a-ḥed ya-kum l'-hi-ga – el.

Fine

D. C. al Fine

95

S'vivon, Sov, Sov, Sov

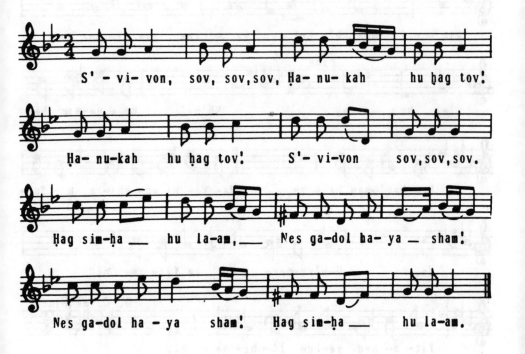

S' - vi- von, sov, sov, sov, Ḥa- nu- kah hu ḥag tov!

Ḥa- nu- kah hu ḥag tov! S' - vi- von sov, sov, sov.

Ḥag sim-ḥa __ hu la-am, __ Nes ga-dol ha- ya __ sham!

Nes ga-dol ha - ya sham! Ḥag sim-ḥa __ hu la-am.

Hanukkah in Photographs

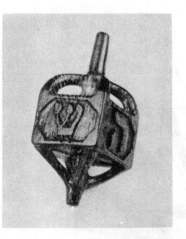

Dreydels are made in many shapes and of various materials. This one, of wood, is an Eastern European 19th-century dreydel.

A very unusual menorah for seven and six lights, made in Morocco or Libya, 18th century.

A terra cotta oil lamp (Palestine, 3rd century, C.E.) showing the columns of the Temple.

Happy boys and girls in a Jewish school, participate in a Hanukkah candle-lighting ceremony.

This is Mod'in, the birthplace of the Maccabees.

The Great Synagogue in Tel Aviv displays a Hanukkah menorah during the eight-day celebration.

Ancient Hebrew coins from the Hasmonean period to the Bar Kochba war. *Bottom row:* "Holy Jerusalem" inscribed on a silver shekel with three pomegranates (68 C.E.).

A Hanukkah menorah stands proudly silhouetted against the sky in Israel.

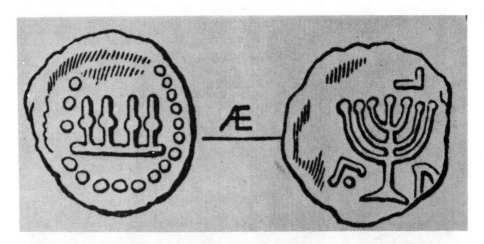

Bronze coin from the reign of Antigonus Mattathias (40-37 B.C.E.). This is the first known appearance of the candle-stick symbol.

A carved menorah in a rock-cut tomb at Bet Shearim, a central burial place for Jews in the 2nd to 4th centuries.

A very rare menorah of about the 9th century. The triangular trough for the shammas candle shows that this is a Hanukkah menorah.

Hanukkah is not complete without a jolly dreydel-spinning game. *Nun, gimel, hay,* and *shin,* are the Hebrew letters on the Hanukkah top.

The story of Judith as told in a 14th century manuscript poem, in Hebrew.

Alexander the Great, king of Macedonia (336-323 B.C.E.).

Glossary

ALEXANDER THE GREAT—King of Macedonia and Greece from 336 B.C.E. to 323 B.C.E. During his twelve-year reign he conquered the near east, western Asia and North Africa.

ANTIOCHUS III—called Antiochus the Great. The father of Antiochus Epiphanes, he was King of Syria from 223 B.C.E. to 187 B.C.E. In 198 B.C.E. he seized Judea from Egypt.

ANTIOCHUS IV—called Antiochus Epiphanes. He was King of Syria from 175 B.C.E. to 163 B.C.E. A cruel and despotic ruler he tried to destroy the Jewish religion and desecrated the Temple. Judah Maccabee led the revolt against him.

APOCRYPHA—A Greek name for ancient books of religious or historical significance, not included in the Bible.

APPOLONIUS—Syrian general who was defeated by Judah Maccabee. Thereafter Judah used his sword in battle.

BETHSURA—A city in ancient Judea. It was here that Judah Maccabee defeated the Syrian forces for the fourth time. After this victory he marched into Jerusalem, cleansed the Temple and celebrated the first Hanukkah.

BOOK OF MACCABEES, THE FIRST—A book of the Apocrypha, it is a historical record of the wars of the Maccabees and the events which led to the uprising.

BOOK OF MACCABEES, THE SECOND—A book of the Apocrypha, it contains inspiring legends and religious writings relating to the Maccabean revolt.

DREYDEL—A four-sided top used in a game played during Hannukah. It is a game of put and take. Using pennies or nuts every participant puts one into the "pot". The children then take turns spinning the dreydel. If it comes to Nun (N), the player gets nothing; Gimel (G) the player takes all; Heh (H), he takes half; Shin (Sh) he puts one in. These four letters refer to the Hebrew words "Nes Gadol Hayah Sham" which means, a great miracle happened there.

GALILEE—The northern district of ancient Palestine and modern day Israel.

GORGIAS—Syrian general defeated by the Maccabean soldiers at Emmaus.

HALLEL—Psalms of praise and thanksgiving recited on Hanukkah.

HANNAH—a martyr whose story is told in the Second Book of Maccabees. This brave mother lived during the reign of Antiochus Epiphanes. Her seven sons bravely gave their lives rather than forsake their Jewish heritage.

HANUKKAH—Literally means "dedication". A holiday commemorating the liberation and the rededication of the ancient

Temple in Jerusalem by Judah Maccabee and his followers.

HANUKKAH GELT—Hanukkah money, sometimes given instead of presents on Hanukkah.

HASMONEANS—Also called Maccabees, descendants of Hashmon, great-grandfather of Mattathias who with his five sons, the Maccabees, led the revolt against Antiochus. Judah was the leader of the Maccabees. After Judah's death his brother Simon became the head of Judea and high priest, thus founding the Hasmonean dynasty in the Kingdom of Judea.

HELLENISM—The ideas, religion and way of life of the ancient Greeks, carried and propagated throughout the ancient world by Alexander the Great.

HOLOFERNES—A legendary general, who according to the Book of Judith in the Aprocrypha, threatened to overcome Jerusalem and destroy Judea. Judith, a beatutiful widow of Jerusalem went to Holofernes camp and said that she had deserted her people. After a drinking party when Holofernes had fallen asleep, Judith killed him and thereby saved her people.

JASON—Greek-loving brother of Onias the high priest, appointed by Antiochus to succeed Onias.

JERUSALEM—Capital of Judea, the Holy City and Site of the Temple.

JEZREEL, VALLEY OF—A beautiful valley cutting across Israel between the mountains of Galilee in the north and the mountains of Samaria in the south. Once a swamp, it is now green and fertile and is heavily dotted with thriving settlements.

JOHN—Oldest son of Mattathias, a brother of Judah Maccabee. One of the leaders of the revolt against Antiochus.

JONATHAN—Fifth son of Mattathias, a brother of Judah Maccabee. After Judah's death, Jonathan became leader of the Jewish forces.

JOSHUA—Hebrew name of Jason.

JUDAH MACCABEE—Leader of the Maccabean revolt. One of five sons of Mattathias, he led the Judeans to victory and rededicated the Temple which the Syrians had desecrated.

JUDEA—Southern half of Palestine. Originally part of a united Kingdom. Under Rehoboam, son of Solomon, the Kingdom split into two kingdoms: Israel in the north and Judea in the south. In 721 B.C. Israel was conquered by the Assyrians and the inhabitants were dispersed. After this catastrophe Judea alone remained of the twelve tribes who had settled in Palestine.

JUDITH—Heroine of a legend of the same name in the Apocrypha. It relates the story of Judith, a beautiful widow of Jerusalem who saved the fortress from destruction by killing the enemy general, Holofernes.

KISLEV—The Hebrew month during which Hanukkah is celebrated. Hanukkah falls on the 25th day of Kislev, which corresponds to the month of December in the Gregorian calendar.

KNESSET—The Hebrew name of the Israeli Parliament.

LATKES—Delicious potato pancakes served during Hanukkah.

MACCABEES—Five sons of the Hasmonean priest Mattathias, heroes of the Maccabean victory over Antiochus. This name has also referred to the guerrila forces which became an army and fought the Syrians.

MAOZ-TSUR—Hebrew name for Rock of Ages, a hymn sung at Hanukkah. The melody dates back to a German song of the 16th Century.

MATTATHIAS—Hasmonean priest of Modin, father of the five Maccabees. He inspired the victorious revolt against Antiochus Epiphanes.

MENORAH—An eight-branched candelabrum with an extra branch, called the "Shammas" which is used to kindle the other lights. The menorah is lit in commemoration of the jug of oil that burned for eight days and nights after the cleansing of the Temple.

MODIN—Village in the Judean hills, home of the Hasmonean priest Mattathias and his five sons. The Maccabean revolt started in Modin.

NEBUCHADNEZZAR—King of Babylonia who defeated Judea in 586 B.C.E. and exiled most of its inhabitants to Babylonia.

NES GADOL HAYAH SHAM—This Hebrew expression means "a great miracle happened there," and refers to the rededication of the ancient Temple in Jerusalem, when it was liberated by Judah Maccabee and his army. The first letter of each word appears on the four sides of the dreydel.

NICANOR—Syrian general defeated by the Maccabean forces at Emmaus.

PTOLEMY—A general of Alexander the Great. After the emperor's death he took over the rule of Egypt.

SELEUCUS—A general of Alexander the Great. After Alexander's death he seized Syria and there established the Seleucid dynasty.

SEPTUAGINT—The first Greek translation of the Bible. It was prepared by a group of scholars in Alexandria in the third century B.C.E. The Septuagint enabled non-Jews and Jews living in the Greek world, who did not know Hebrew, to read the Bible. The Septuagint is a Greek word meaning "translation of the 70".

SERON—Syrian general defeated by the Maccabees.

SHAMMAS—The "helper" candle used to light the other eight candles of the Hanukkah menorah.

SIMON—Second son of Mattathias, the Hasmonean. Last of the five brothers to survive the struggle for independence. In his time Judea became an independent kingdom.

SYRIA—State to the north of Judea. Once part of the Macedonian Empire it was seized by Seleucus, one of Alexander's generals. Antiochus Epiphanes was King of Syria.

ZECHARIAH—Last King of Judea before the Babylonian exile.

ZEUS—Chief god of the Greeks.

Bibliography

Apocrypha, The: Translated out of the Greek and Latin tongues, Oxford University Press, London: Humphrey Milford, 1926.

Atlas of the Bible — L. H. Grollenberg, O.P., Translated and edited by Joyce M. H. Reid, and H. H. Romley, Thomas Nelson and Sons, Ltd., London and Edinburgh, 1956.

Bialostotzky, B. J.: "Fun undzer Oytser", mayses un legendes, Fun Golus Bovel Biz Roym, Central Yiddish Culture Organization, Inc., New York, 1949.

Bickerman, Elias: The Maccabees — An Account of their History From the Beginnings to the Fall of the House of the Hasmoneans, Schocken Books, New York, 1947.

Coopersmith, Harry. The Songs We Sing, The United Synagogue Commission on Education, New York, 1950.

Epstein, Morris: All About Jewish Holidays and Customs, Ktav Publishing House, Inc., New York, 1959.

Fast, Howard: My Glorious Brothers, Little Brown and Co., New York, 1948.

First Book of Maccabees, the Commentary by H. A. Fischel, Schocken Books, New York, 1948.

Gaster Theodor H.: Festivals of the Jewish Year. A modern interpretation and guide, William Sloan Associates Publishers, New York, 1952.

Gilbert, Arthur and Tarcov, Oscar: Your Neighbor Celebrates — Jewish Holidays and traditions in America, Friendly House Publishers, New York, 1957.

Goldin, Hyman E.: The Jew and His Duties, The Essence of the Kitzur Shulhan Arukh, ethically presented, Hebrew Publishing Company, 1953.

Grayzel, Solomon: A History of the Jews, from the Babylonian Exile to the end of World War II, The Jewish Publication Society of America, Philadelphia, 1947.

Junior Jewish Cook Book — Aunt Fanny, Ktav Publishing House, New York, 1956.

Kastein, Josef: History and Destiny of the Jews, translated from the German by Huntley Paterson, Garden City Publishing Co., Inc., Garden City, N. Y., 1936.

Levinger, Elma Ehrlich: Chanukah Entertainments, Union of American Hebrew Congregations, New York, 1924.

Myers, Jack K.: The Story of the Jewish People — Being a history of the Jewish people since Bible times, Volume I. Kegan Paul, Trench, Trubner and Co., Ltd. London. The Bloch Publishing Co., New York, 1922.

Roth, Cecil: A Bird's Eye View of Jewish History, Union of American Hebrew Congregations, New York, 1954.

Sachar, Abram Leon: A History of the Jews, Second edition, revised. Alfred A. Knopf, New York, 1940.

Schauss, Hayyim: The Jewish Festivals, Union of American Hebrew Congregations, New York, 1938.

Solis-Cohen, Emily: Hanukkah, The Feast of Lights, The Jewish Publication Society of America, Philadelphia, 1937.

Tarcov, Oscar and Tarcov, Edith: The Illustrated Book of Jewish Knowledge, Friendly House Publishers, New York, 1959.

THE PHOTOGRAPHS